ÆSTHETICS AND LANGUAGE

ÆSTHETICS AND LANGUAGE

Essays by

PROFESSOR W. B. GALLIE

PROFESSOR GILBERT RYLE

BERYL LAKE

PROFESSOR ARNOLD ISENBERG

STUART HAMPSHIRE

PROFESSOR J. A. PASSMORE

PROFESSOR O. K. BOUWSMA

MARGARET MACDONALD

HELEN KNIGHT

PAUL ZIFF

EDITED WITH AN INTRODUCTION BY
WILLIAM ELTON

BASIL BLACKWELL
OXFORD
1967

First printed in this edition 1954

Reprinted 1967

PRINTED IN GREAT BRITAIN BY OFFSET LITHOGRAPHY BY
BILLING AND SONS LTD., GUILDFORD AND LONDON

αὐτὰρ ὑπ' αὐτήν ἐστιν ἀταρπιτὸς ὀκρυόεσσα,
κοίλη, πηλώδης· ἡ δ' ἡγήσασθαι ἀρίστη
ἄλσος ἐς ἱμερόεν πολυτιμήτου Ἀφροδίτης.

DIELS, *Fragmente der Vorsokratiker*,
18. B. Fr. 20.

CONTENTS

ÆSTHETICS AND LANGUAGE

CHAPTER I

INTRODUCTION

By William Elton

THE present collection attempts to diagnose and clarify some æsthetic confusions, which it holds to be mainly linguistic in origin.[1] It employs, for the most part, methods of analysis which prevail in the philosophical faculties of Oxford, Cambridge, and London, as well as in certain academic localities in Australasia and the United States.[2] This anthology is addressed to two classes of readers. First, as little is known of the new developments outside of professional circles and their journals, it intends to make representative essays conveniently accessible to laymen, both general readers as well as those primarily concerned with the theory and practice of the arts. Secondly, it aims to provide philosophers and their students with a number of pieces that may serve as models of analytical procedure in æsthetics. Despite the scarcity of such examples, sufficient able work has appeared to form a book which may stimulate further studies. In selecting these essays, our criteria included freshness of approach, concern with fundamental linguistic confusions, and freedom from the usual obfuscatory jargon. Unfortunately, for reasons of space, we have had to omit some worthwhile pieces, and to their

---

[1] The idea for this volume was suggested by A. G. N. Flew's editions of *Essays on Logic and Language* (Blackwell, First Series, 1951; Second Series, 1953). As similar principles operate in all three cases, in order to save space the reader is referred to Mr. Flew's introductions.

[2] Surveys of recent developments in analytical philosophy include: Morris Weitz' 'Oxford Philosophy', *Philosophical Review*, LXII (1953), 187–233, and Stuart Hampshire's 'Changing Methods in Philosophy', *Philosophy*, XXVI (1951), 142–5; and less technically, John Holloway's 'The "New Philosophy of Language" in England', *Hudson Review*, IV (1951), 448–57. The most seminal influence has been the work of the later Wittgenstein, and an illuminating account is Gilbert Ryle's 'Ludwig Wittgenstein', *Analysis*, XII (1951), 1–9. Fuller bibliographical details, obviating the need for their mention here, will be found in the forthcoming bibliography in preparation by the sub-faculty of philosophy at Oxford.

authors our apologies are due. The arrangement is topical: two
articles on the general field of æsthetics are followed by three on
problems of feeling, emotion, and expression, while the concluding five deal with questions of æsthetic judgment and criticism.
If æsthetics is not the illusory 'Mrs. Harris branch of philosophy', its confusions may be real and abundant. According to
some philosophers, the barrenness of æsthetics is demonstrated
by the fact that, while *Streitschriften* proliferate, progress is rare.[1]
They find evidence, as well, in such *aperçus* as, 'the music of
Lourié is an ontological music; in the Kierkegaardian style, one
would also say "existential". It is born in the singular roots of
being, the nearest possible juncture of the soul and spirit. . . .'
Reviewers of these remarks by an eminent philosopher were,
according to a contributor, so used to nonsense in æsthetical
writings, that even when the translator piled meaninglessness on
meaninglessness, they remained unperturbed. Philosophers sceptical of traditional approaches might hold that the natural home
of rapturous or soporific effusion is the field of æsthetics; and
they might agree when Irving Babbitt describes it as the 'night-
mare science', when John Wisdom mentions its 'dullness', and
J. A. Passmore its 'dreariness', or even when C. D. Broad arraigns
it as 'boring and . . . largely bogus'. They might suggest that it
is boring partly at times because it seems so unprofitable, and
partly at times on account of the striking contrast with the
material it is supposed to illuminate. 'Why', asked William
James, 'does the *Æsthetik* of every German philosopher seem to
the artist like the abomination of desolation?' Whether or not
one concurs in these indictments, and whether or not one agrees
regarding the 'present stone age of æsthetic inquiry',[2] one may

---

[1] P. O. Kristeller, in 'The Modern System of the Arts: A Study in the History of
Aesthetics', *Journal of the History of Ideas*, XII (1951), 496–527, and XIII (1952), 17–46,
emphasizes that much of what we take for granted in æsthetics is of recent origin. The
system of the five 'major arts', for example, was unfamiliar to classical, medieval, and
Renaissance thought, and such ambiguous terms as 'art' and 'beauty' have acquired
additional modern meanings.

[2] Arnold Isenberg, this volume, p. 144. His *Analytical Philosophy and the Study of Art:
A Report to the Rockefeller Foundation* (priv. circ., 1950) is a detailed recommendation for
the application of analytical techniques to æsthetics. Doubts regarding traditional
æsthetics have been expressed by other than analytical philosophers; cf. Santayana's
reference to 'sheer verbiage' and D. W. Prall's to 'pseudo-science or pseudo-philosophy'.
The summary of C. I. Lewis may stand: 'In the whole area of philosophic studies there
is probably no other topic which is marked by so much unclarity and so little unanimity
as is exhibited by the subject of esthetic theory'.

conclude that an inspection of the linguistic foundations of the subject is long overdue.

I. The following essays constitute an initial approach to such an investigation. Although a conspectus of their contents reveals inevitable contradictions on certain points, a summary of what a number of contributors regard as sources of confusion may be found useful. (1) First, with reference to the field of æsthetics itself, the essayists are constrained to warn against the pitfalls of generality. 'Art', no more than 'æsthetics', necessarily stands for any one thing; the presence of a substantive is no guarantee that a single substance exists to correspond with it. The 'craving for generality', of which Wittgenstein speaks, is illustrated by Professor Ryle in the example of a child who fancies that all the MacTavishes in the world must belong to the family of Mac-Tavishes living next door. Rather than works of art sharing common 'æsthetic properties', they share a certain mode of consideration or approach; as Professor Passmore points out, there may be an æsthetic approach, just as there may be a scientific approach, without necessitating that objects have æsthetic or scientific characters. For example, the 'organic' quality of works of art is not a special æsthetic property, necessarily the same in all works of art; it is a category rather than a property, suggesting the kinds of questions to be asked. Furthermore, stretching terms such as 'balance' and 'theme' beyond their function in one art may result in meaninglessness. Illegitimate assimilation of differences and reductionism are consequences of facile generalization. The arts are multiple, and irreducible, with Taine, to naturalistic elements, or with Croce, to imagination or expression. The tendencies sketched above, together with the desire to use art instrumentally as a 'clue to reality', lead to the peculiar dullness, pretentiousness, and woolliness characteristic of æsthetic writing. The arts, in short, differ greatly among themselves, and it is incorrect to say that art is craft, or art is moral or amoral. (2) The tendency to generality is connected with the predisposition to essentialism, or the belief that there is one essence or ultimate nature present in an object, and that to understand that object one must first grasp its essence. This knowledge of essences is assumed to be derived by methods different from those used in empirical, mathematical, or common-sense operations. As

Professor Gallie indicates, essentialist, Idealist thinking holds that there is one meaning, one reading, and one act of creation in connexion with a work of art; that the reading is identical with the creation; and that art is one mode of 'Spirit'. It holds that there is one thing known as 'the tragic', 'the epic', etc. However, both generality and essentialism can be shown to have fruitless or misleading consequences. Insistence upon the 'rules' and upon mark-giving is similarly futile, and a cause of dullness in æsthetics. (3) Misleading analogies are another source of confusion in the field. Examples are such correspondences among the arts as 'the music of poetry', as well as ambiguous uses of such terms as 'balance' with regard to more than one art. Another sort of misleading analogy, according to Mr. Hampshire, is that with ethics, and is basic to the misconception of the role of æsthetics. Questioning the 'Alexandrianism' which requires that every subject-name have a subject-matter behind it, he attempts to show that the subject-matter of æsthetics may have been derived, by a *petitio principii*, from the analogy with ethics. He argues that æsthetic judgments are not comparable with moral judgments, the work of art being gratuitous, unpractical, particular, and unique. Mr. Hampshire believes that, if his premises are correct, they would explain the poverty of much æsthetic writing—books, for example, which are completed in order to round out a philosophical system and with no clear understanding of the proper range of subject-matter. Other instances of misleading analogy include the one with science, which Dr. Macdonald and Professor Isenberg are concerned to dispute; the consequences of this type of error will be considered below. (4) Generality, essentialism, and misleading analogies help to account for the condition of the subject. But Miss Lake indicates another peculiar feature of æsthetics, the tautologous, *a priori* nature of some, if not all, of its theories. Analysing two samples, Croce's 'Art is expression', and Bell's 'Art is significant form', she finds them to be irrefutable and non-empirical. Differing from other types of statements, they are a result of the desire to emphasize one fact about æsthetic objects to the exclusion of others; they thus resemble such remarks as 'the only universities in England are Oxford and Cambridge', where the observer refuses to recognize anything else as a university.

II. In considering the important role of such terms as 'feeling', 'emotion', and 'expression' in æsthetics, we encounter a vexing welter of ambiguities. Patiently unravelling some of the senses of 'feeling', Professor Ryle traces unnoticed transferences of meaning from one sense to another. Especially significant, however, are the uses of 'feeling' in æsthetic contexts. Intuition, a faculty parallel to Sense and Reason in the theorizing of some philosophers, is shown by the author in this and similar instances to be a special case of feeling ('feeling that something is the case') rather than a separate faculty. Influenced likewise by tripartitionism, theorists have assimilated 'feeling-that' to 'emotion', *e.g.* expressions of the type 'possessing a particular flair' being confused with expressions of the type 'having fear'. Through some such assimilation, the artist is alleged to have an 'emotion' when he creates, and if he is skilful, the audience is supposed to be infected with that emotion. As he works, the artist's 'emotion' may in truth be boredom, absorption, or jealousy, but the theorist insists on conferring upon him some emotion or other, or, at least, a recollection of some emotion. And Professor Ryle notes that sometimes nameless æsthetic emotions are invoked in order to make the theory respectable. In her essay, Dr. Macdonald reveals similar doubts about whether the artist expresses emotional states, and wonders how it is possible for a critic to determine whether he has correctly reproduced the emotional state of an artist.

Closely related to 'feeling' is 'expression', and Professor Bouwsma undertakes to expose the ambiguities and inadequacies in the widely-held expression theory of art. In his method, he follows Wittgenstein's counsel that an important way to discover the meaning of a term is to ask how, and in what contexts, it is employed, *i.e. what would it be like* for music to express sadness? He concludes that sadness is not a separable entity which is 'expressed'; the sadness is in the music, just as character is in a face, or life is in a squirrel. Two misleading contexts determine the use of 'expression': (1) the language of emotion (emotion is a kind of stored liquid which is ready to be tapped and poured forth, *e.g.* 'poetry is the spontaneous overflow of powerful emotions' suggests stored emotions ready to be tapped; the Aristotelian notion of catharsis is an example of the misleading liquid-emotion analogy); and (2) the language of language (a sentence is like a doorbell which buzzes, and arouses or evokes ideas; here, too, the idea is supposed to be stored up, in some inner world, waiting to be expressed). In the defence of the expression theory, there is a strategic shift from the first context to the second, in order to preserve its plausibility. Music is then said to express sadness (or art to express emotion) as sentences express (or evoke) ideas. A puzzling feature about the analogy that music evokes emotions as sentences evoke images is that, while the former sometimes occurs, it often does not, as when the sadness of the listener is dry-eyed; the analogy is therefore both correct and misleading. It may make sense, moreover, to ask what a sentence expresses, and to demand that it be put into other words, but it makes no sense to ask what a poem expresses. The emotions are in the poem's words as you hear them; the poem expresses no emotions at all. If we say 'the music is sad', we should be careful about going on to the misleading 'the music expresses sadness'. Although her aims are different, Miss Lake also criticizes the expression theory by showing it to be, in Croce's hands, analytic and non-empirical.

III. Further attack upon the Crocean and Idealist *mythos*, which writers in this book generally oppose, involves questioning of the notion that the art-object does not really exist, the work of art being not really physical; *i.e.* the material object is merely the occasion, or the point of departure, for an imaginative construction, which is the genuine work of art. Professor Gallie suggests that this subjectivism is the result of a confusion between the value we attribute to a work of art and its existence. Valuing belongs to the creator and the enjoyer, he affirms, but, as other contributors would agree, it does not follow that both types of valuing are identical. The reduction of the work of art to its mere imaginative creation is implausible, he urges, as the pigments, stone, etc., do contribute to our enjoyment, and as, moreover, new materials and instruments in the history of art have determined the direction of artistic inspiration. According to Miss Lake, however, defenders of the Idealist position, such as Croce, might admit Professor Gallie's contentions, and still insist that the art-work is subjective, arguing that the material object is a mere occasion or initiating point for the real work of art. But Miss Lake shows that Croce's position is not empirical, because it would be impossible to present him with a set of instances which might disprove his theory; there is no way to prove him true or false, as there might be to disprove 'All works of art are paintings', by pointing to sculpture, and then to the dictionary and common usage. Although Croce apparently wishes to restrict 'Art' to the kinds of intuitions he describes, this is contrary to normal usage.

Nevertheless, it does not follow from the opposition to Croce's theory that the work of art is merely the uninterpreted material object. As Dr. Macdonald indicates, works of art are esoteric and complex, different from other types of things, as well as from their own material embodiment. The latter is certainly an essential part of the work, *pace* the Croceans; without it, there would be no work. But if a work of art is not a physical object, Dr. Macdonald observes, it needn't therefore be a mental state. Without wishing to be taken too literally, she suggests that a work of art is not an object but a manner of speaking. (This is not far from Professor Passmore's denial that there is a set of entities called 'æsthetic experiences'.) And she holds that the problem is not of what kinds of objects exist, but of how words are used. With regard to non-physical works of art, such as poems, plays, and musical compositions, she asserts, there is no object which is the real work apart from some interpretation. The object cannot be that which existed in the mind of the composer, as nothing can restore that to us. Nor is it possible to restore the *Hamlet* of Shakespeare's audience to us. The art object, she says, is not identifiable like a pebble, but is more like a set of variations, of which none is the 'real' one. 'Same' in 'same work of art' is used analogously to its employment in the 'same function'. Her own reading of *Hamlet*, she remarks, is but one of a group of more-or-less similar performances, without which it would not make sense to speak of the play. The idea of the 'work-in-itself' which is inexperienceable is a myth; but the interpretations of the work are uniquely connected in its construction. Like others in the volume, Dr. Ziff is concerned to demolish the Idealist view that the work of art is a mental state, and that when we talk about a work of art we do not discuss a painting, but some illusory or imaginary thing. By showing the differences between a mirage or hallucination and the effects, *e.g.* of depth, which he holds are really in the painting and not an illusion, he attempts to dispose of the Idealist view. Again, it is a problem of the way in which we speak of the work of art, rather than of the object. He concludes that distinctions are more properly drawn between various descriptions, rather than various objects.

IV. The process of the criticism and evaluation of works of art involves a number of linguistic problems. For example, the meaning of 'good' in the sentence 'this work is good', is discussed by Dr. Knight, Dr. Macdonald, and Professor Passmore. Dr. Knight states that the meaning of 'beauty' would involve similar puzzles. To say that a work is good is not the same as to say that one likes it; one could meaningfully affirm that one knows that a work of art is good, despite the fact that one confesses one doesn't like it. According to Dr. Knight, the goodness of a work of art is analogous to the goodness of a tennis player, a Pekingese dog, or a steak; goodness depends on the criteria of goodness in each of these cases. It is plausible to assert that one's desire for an experience is a criterion for its goodness, but it is implausible to conclude that any of one's mental states is a criterion for the goodness of a particular tennis player. Returning to the work of art, to say that a painting is good is not to use 'good' in a general sense, but in one of a number of specific senses; the goodness of the painting depends on its possession of criterion-characters. The criteria are diverse, being sometimes one set and sometimes another, and the sets overlap, offering different combinations. It follows that the comparison of paintings which are good for different reasons would in some cases be nonsensical; it would be like asking whether rugged scenery is better than soft. Nevertheless, if comparisons between works whose criteria differ do occur, that is because some criteria are judged higher than others. The guarantee that something is a criterion of goodness lies in its being used as such. While it is true that criteria for artistic goodness are not fixed like the points for judging a dog, it is misleading to suggest that they are not fixed at all. Much æsthetic disagreement is disagreement in the use of the word 'good'; *i.e.* different criteria are involved, although the parties to the dispute may agree on the nature of what they are discussing. Further, since fixing criteria and their employment are two different things, in applying criteria we are not concerned with the circumstances in which they have been fixed.

While Professor Passmore agrees to a large extent with these remarks by Dr. Knight, Dr. Macdonald finds herself unable to accept them, for two reasons: (1) works of art being unique, it is difficult to conceive of them as tying for first place by virtue of a set of criteria-characters, or by listing their characteristics and supposing them to add up to the same sum; and (2) it is difficult to conceive of a work of art as a cake whose meritorious features might be picked out and exhibited. Dr. Macdonald would reject this as a model of the work of art, on the grounds that the critic's task seems never to be finished, interpretation and evaluation being a continuous process. To suppose that works are simple objects whose features can be presented for listing, is to be misled by the methods of science; in science, time and place do not affect the result, whether objects are observed here, now, or were observed centuries ago, in another country. Works of art, however, are constantly being reinterpreted, and there seems to be no work apart from some interpretation. Another misleading scientific analogy consists in the notion that there is a general 'theory' behind individual criticisms; this use of 'theory' assumes, by analogy with scientific method, that from observation of a selection of works of art, critics construct a theoretical standard to which all artists must conform, and by which their works may be judged. After further observation and the emergence of contrary instances, one supersedes the previous hypothesis by a new one. However, it is wrong to think of one poet or style being superseded by another, in the manner that one scientific theory replaces another. New facts, in the case of works of art, do not affect interpretations in the same way as do new facts in the case of scientific theories. Similarly, factual investigations into the mental processes of either artist or members of his audience are irrelevant, since criticism is not an empirical, psychological exercise. A work of art is not a state of mind, nor the effect of such a state combined with technical ability in the medium.[1] Further distinctions between works of art and science include the fact that, while a decision regarding art is reached by a definite procedure, it is unlike the scientific process of moving from evidence to conclusion in deductive or inductive inference. Rather than the activity of scientists or logicians, critical evaluations of art resemble the procedure of law courts, show rings, and selection boards. Dr. Macdonald goes on to affirm that verdicts and awards in artistic judgments are not true or false, in so far as they may be reversed but not disproved; no one can be argued into liking a work, and deductive and inductive methods do not apply. Art being creation, rather than discovery, criticism and appraisal resemble creation more than demonstration or proof. Resembling the occupation of the actor and executant, rather than that of the scientist or logician, the critic's task is comparable to that of a lawyer who 'creates' his client's case from the 'facts'. But, curiously, the critic differs from the counsellor in that he is also the judge of what he presents. Since some construction must precede judgment, the critic is 'creative'. The verdict he delivers does not name a simple quality, nor a simple feeling in the critic; 'this is good' also has the form of the impersonal verdict, 'he is guilty'. While the verdict does not describe the accused or express the feelings of the judge, it affirms a decision reached by a definite procedure. The justification of the critical verdict, Dr. Macdonald concludes, is not a result of measuring the judgment against a mythical 'real' work of art independent of interpretation, but the outcome of an appraisal in relation to the qualities of the critic, *e.g.* his experience, skill, etc. Criticism is, in short, an indefinite series of methods for 'presenting', rather than proving, the values of a work of art.

These observations of Dr. Macdonald are supported by Professor Passmore's belief that what a work 'means' depends on what it suggests to a particular observer, rather than upon any 'essence' hidden within it. Likewise, Professor Isenberg carries

---

[1] Cf. W. K. Wimsatt, Jr., and Monroe Beardsley, who have argued against confusions between the mind or 'intention' of the creator and his work, on the one hand, and between the work and its effect on the audience, on the other hand, in 'The Intentional Fallacy', *Sewanee Review*, LIV (1946), 468–88, and 'The Affective Fallacy', ibid., LVII (1949), 31–55. See further, on the status of the 'art object', M. Macdonald, 'Art and Imagination', *Proc. Aristotelian Soc.*, n.s. LIII (1953), 205–26; and, on distinctions between scientific and critical models, Herbert Dingle, *Science and Literary Criticism*, London, Nelson, 1949.

forward Dr. Macdonald's opposition to misleading scientific analogies in discussions of art. Mainly, he is concerned to distinguish the peculiar quality of critical communication from other types of communication. Whereas, in ordinary communication, symbols may have a significance independent of sense-perception, a function of criticism is to effect communication at the level of the senses, *i.e.* to bring about a similarity of experienced content. Reading criticism apart from the presence or direct recollection of the work of art is a worthless undertaking, if we take the peculiar nature of critical communication into account. Distinguishing criticism further from misleading scientific analogies, Professor Isenberg emphasizes that criticism is not committed to the general claim that a work is good by virtue of the presence of a particular quality; the truth of the specific reason for the critical verdict adds nothing to the verdict, because the specific reason designates no quality the perception of which might lead us to concur in the verdict. And if it is not the specific reason that makes the verdict acceptable, it is clear that the reason cannot possibly require the support of the general, or theoretical, norm or principle that any work which has that quality is to that extent good. But critics and readers often are misled into believing that criticism makes the claim that a work is good because it has a particular quality. This claim implies that a critic abandons his own role to pose as a scientist, and assumes that criticism explains experiences instead of clarifying and altering them.

From the summaries here set forth, it is clear that the contributors share many general attitudes without necessarily agreeing on all points. It is obvious, too, that as a number of these essays were written some time ago, they may not always represent the authors' present views; nor, of course, do they necessarily reflect those of the editor. While it is difficult to affix on to these essayists a general label, and certainly incorrect to associate them with positivism or other dogmatic, procrustean attitudes toward meaningfulness, one may say that they share the climate of analysis to which such men as Gottlob Frege, Bertrand Russell, G. E. Moore, and, especially, Ludwig Wittgenstein contributed. Wittgenstein, whose mark is on some, though not all, of the contributors, held, for example, that we tend to mistake a syntactically correct sentence for a necessarily meaningful one;

B

that language resembles a game, and that there are numerous such games, depending on the particular uses of language;[1] that we have a 'craving for generality' which misleads us; that we tend to employ analogies which mislead us;[2] that philosophy, in short, is not a body of dogma, but the examination of the ways in which language is used.

We wish to thank those who made this volume possible: the authors for kindly consenting to the reproduction of their papers; and the editors and publishers who first issued the essays, for graciously permitting their republication. Chapters II, III, and XI appeared originally in *Mind* for 1948 and 1951; Chapter VII in Supplementary Volume XXIII of the *Proceedings of the Aristotelian Society* and Chapter IX in the same *Proceedings* for 1949; Chapter IV in the *Philosophical Quarterly* for 1951; Chapter VIII in the *Philosophical Review* for 1949; and Chapter X in the *World Review* for 1952. Chapter VI, here published for the first time, is part of a dissertation completed at Smith College under the direction of Professors Morris and Alice Lazerowitz. Chapter V was part of a collection entitled *Philosophical Analysis*, edited by Max Black (Cornell University Press, 1950). Finally, we should like to express our gratitude to the many philosophers who have encouraged and counselled our project from the very start, and to acknowledge the assistance of a few people who have aided in many ways: Professor O. K. Bouwsma, C. O. Burgess, Professor Arnold Isenberg, Professor S. F. Johnson, Dr. Margaret Macdonald, and Professor R. H. Pearce. The present book was undertaken during the editor's tenure of a Scholar's Award from the American Council of Learned Societies.

---

[1] See his posthumously published work, *Philosophical Investigations* (trans. G. E. M. Anscombe, Blackwell, 1953), pp. 11–12, 224. It is this effort, rather than the earlier *Tractatus Logico-Philosophicus*, that represents the views which have now the greatest influence. On Wittgenstein, cf., in addition to the article by Ryle, *supra*, J. N. Findlay, 'Wittgenstein's Philosophic Investigations', *Revue Internationale de Philosophie*, 1953, pp. 201–16; D.A.T.G. and A.C.J., 'Ludwig Wittgenstein', *Australasian Journal of Philosophy*, XXIX (1951), 73–80; John Wisdom in *Mind*, LXI (1952), 258–60, and *Philosophy and Psycho-Analysis* (Blackwell, 1953); and the review of the later work, by P. F. Strawson, *Mind*, LXIII (1954), 70–99. By 'language-game' should be understood no trivial view of language; Wittgenstein used the term analogically, to cast light on the complex family of activities which come under the head of 'using language', as well as on the rules which are employed.

[2] *Phil. Inves.*, p. 151.

CHAPTER II

THE FUNCTION OF PHILOSOPHICAL ÆSTHETICS

By W. B. Gallie

Introductory. In this paper I attempt three things: first, a fairly close examination of the underlying assumptions and characteristic results of Idealist æsthetics; second, on the basis of my criticism of these, a re-statement of the function and method of æsthetics; and thirdly, one fairly detailed illustration of what I take that function and method to be.

I adopt this procedure for two reasons. In the first place the Idealist doctrine that Art is, essentially, Imagination has dominated philosophical æsthetics for the last hundred and fifty years, and during this period the vocabulary and presuppositions of artistic and literary criticism—from which any philosophical æsthetics must draw its raw material—have been profoundly affected by this Idealist doctrine. Consequently, in order to deal completely to-day with philosophical problems arising from criticism, one must be equipped to distinguish the critic's relatively direct judgments and appreciations from their Idealist accretions. This is my main reason for approaching my subject historically— from nineteenth-century Idealist theories. But secondly, I believe that these theories are well worth investigating because they illustrate, in their own way so strikingly, certain very pervasive philosophical fallacies and confusions. For instance, I believe that they are vitiated through and through by the 'essentialist fallacy': they presuppose, that is, that whenever we are in a position to define a substance or activity we must know its essence or ultimate nature—and know this by methods that are entirely different from those used in the experimental and mathematical sciences or in our common-sense judgments about minds and material things. Now, is their subjection to this fallacy a reason for consigning Idealist æsthetics to oblivion?

Anyone urging this would, I suggest, do well to remember how tenacious and seductive a doctrine essentialism has proved to be. He would do well to recall how many of the greatest philosophers since Descartes have devoted perhaps their best energies to exposing essentialist fallacies, only to slip back—as soon as their philosophic interest flags or their acquaintance with relevant scientific procedures is defective—into unmistakably essentialist habits of thought. For essentialism is not only deep-rooted in man's thought habits—or linguistic habits; as it penetrates different departments of human thought it works on these, at first stimulating them but eventually blunting or distorting them, in markedly different ways. This is why the abandonment of essentialist habits of thought in mechanics did not lead automatically to the abandonment of them in other parts of physics, or in biology, psychology, and the political and social sciences. On the contrary, in each of these disciplines a fresh diagnosis of essentialist errors has been (or still is) needed, and a fresh act of excision. To attempt such a diagnosis in the field of æsthetics is, then, neither otiose nor trivial; and the act of excision which it demands can help us to see how at least some problems of æsthetics, confused in the Idealist treatment, can be posed in manageable—answerable—form.

Idealist Æsthetics. Consider the following statements:

(A) There is *one* way of reading a particular poem, and this gives us that poem's individual meaning and value. (For poem one could substitute painting, musical composition, or what not.)

(B) There is (or was) *one* act of Imagination which also makes (or made) that poem's individual meaning and value.

(c) The 'reading' referred to in (A) and the 'act' referred to in (B) are, despite historical and psychological differences (accidents), 'ideally identical': they are equivalent conditions of the existence, meaning, and value of the poem.

(D) The material embodiment of any poem, painting, or what not is *æsthetically* irrelevant: the poem exists, as a poem, in the imaginative 'act' or 'reading'.

(E) There is one way of explaining the 'reading' referred to in (A), the 'act' referred to in (B), and the 'identity' referred to in (C): and this understanding gives us the essence of what poetry in general—or, for that matter, of what Art in general—is.

(F)   This explanation or concept of the essence of Art inevitably leads us to see the need of other equally general concepts of the essence of, e.g., history, science, morality, religion, philosophy, and so on. In other words, to understand Art means to see it as one 'mode' or 'category' or 'grade' of 'Spirit'.

These statements are intended simply as reminders of some of the main tenets of Idealist theories. If I have slightly over-simplified any of them this hardly matters, so long as the reader recalls the kind of tenet that is in question. For what I want chiefly to consider is the *logical order* in which these tenets stand in Idealist theories.

To anyone whose thoughts are guided by empiricist principles it would seem obvious that the later statements in this list, especially (E) and (F), must owe whatever plausibility they have to the truth or probability of the earlier statements, and that these, especially (A) and (B), must be based on a very careful investigation of the objects, activities, and enjoyments which ordinary language brackets together as 'Art'. Idealist philosophers, on the other hand, seem to me, without exception, to argue for these earlier statements, (A) to (D), on the assumption that statements (E) and (F) *must* be true, indeed, to philosophical reflexion, are *obviously* true. Their arguments in favour of statements (A) to (D) are, very broadly, eliminative: suggested alternatives to statements (A) to (D) are shown—on the assumption that (E) and (F) are true—to be confused and self-contradictory or such that they 'collapse into identity'—*i.e.* into statement (D) or (C) or (B) or (A).[1] I would not, of course, deny that Idealist æstheti-cians have tried hard to square the consequences of their initial tenets with the relevant facts of artistic creation and enjoyment. To be sure, I do not find their efforts successful: but in fairness to

[1] The justice of this account can readily be proved by recalling the lay-out of Collingwood's *The Philosophy of Art*, or of ch. iii of Croce's *Æsthetic*, or chs. xii and xiv of the *Biographia Literaria*. Interesting historical and psychological evidence as to the first infection of modern æsthetics by essentialist ways of thinking can be found in the autobiographical writings of Vico and Coleridge. (See Vico's *Autobiography*, Part A, 1725; and *Biographia Literaria*, chs. v to ix.)

them, one must, I think, trace out their failure from the basic statements (E) and (F).

The most important fact about these two statements is that by conjoining them Idealist æstheticians have absolved themselves from facing a prior question: namely, what reasons have we for thinking that the word Art stands for some *one* thing. Two purely logical considerations are pertinent here. (i) Our use of an abstract word such as 'Art' does not necessarily imply something common to all the objects we apply it to. Such a word might stand for a group of entities between whose every member and *at least two others* there hold two *different* relations of likeness (or relations of likeness in two different respects). This would be enough to justify our use of the word in 'blanket' fashion. The phrase 'family resemblance' is the eponymic instance, in modern logical theory, of words of this sort: the word 'play' provides another instance. (ii) Even when all the instances of an abstract word have something in common, it by no means follows that this something is the most important feature of each instance of that word or the feature in virtue of which we most readily understand each instance. Think, for instance, of the word 'king'. A king is always male: but in different ages to be a king has meant to be now a priest, now a war-leader, now a sovereign or supreme executive, now a constitutional servant. Now it seems to me, in view of the bewildering variety of objects and activities that have been prized as art in different civilizations and in different ages, that the word 'Art' may well be of the sort described in (i) above. And even if we confine attention to limited periods, it seems certain to me that the word 'Art', as used within such limited periods, is often of the sort described in (ii) above. More positively, there are such things as *revolutions* in artistic taste and inspiration, and after such a revolution certain things are classified as Art which were not before, while other things are no longer classified as Art.

How is it that Idealist æstheticians, most of them scrupulous historians of art and artistic ideas, have failed to ask themselves whether the word 'Art' in fact stands for some *one* thing? The explanation goes back to their initial view: that there is one total Spiritual Activity (or Notion or Logos), and that Art is one of the distinguishable grades or categories in which it acts. The metaphysical, monistic and mentalist, character of this view is quite as important as its logical, essentialist, character (the former is in fact a special case of the latter, being derived from the senseless statement that *Esse* is essentially *percipi* or *intelligi*). Granted, however, that this view were meaningful and true, it would follow that our initial question was redundant, and the autonomy of philosophical æsthetics within an Idealist philosophy would be ensured. The job of philosophical æsthetics would be to articulate the essence of Art as one grade of Spirit (this means, as a rule, equating it with Imaginative activity) and to exclude from the category of Art those features, ordinarily ascribed to works of art or to artistic creation or enjoyment, which cannot be comprised within this essence or equation. But how can this procedure be squared with a recognition of revolutions in artistic taste and inspiration? Quite easily—granted the truth of statements (E) and (F). For we can then claim that such revolutions are only *clarifications* of men's single, though too often blurred, conception of what Art is, or that such revolutions, although of great consequence to Art, do not affect its essence. (For example, history opens up new subject-matters, or technology provides new material mediums, for art, and the resulting revolution in artistic interests may be enormous. But since neither subject-matter nor material medium belongs to the essence of Art, it isn't (essentially) an 'artistic revolution'.)

Such, in briefest outline, is the genesis of Idealist æsthetics; let us now turn to its consequences as expressed in statements (A) to (D). Here again we might naturally expect that the somewhat paradoxical statements (C) and (D) have been put forward to account for some unsuspected feature of artistic creation and enjoyment which a close examination of these has disclosed. But statements (C) and (D) are virtually necessitated by the initial tenets which we have just discussed, and in so far as they are supported by an examination of relevant fact this is a very one-sided affair, aimed only too obviously at 'saving the appearances'.

If we begin with the assumption that Art is essentially one grade or activity of Spirit, then we are faced with some pretty obvious difficulties. For, to common sense, the word 'Art' suggests a complex situation in which three distinct factors are

involved: artist or artistic activity, works of art, and the enjoyment of works of art. Idealist æsthetics, given its initial assumptions is committed to reducing this triadic situation to unity—
to monadic *act* (Art being, by definition, a grade or activity of
Spirit). The required reduction is made first by eliminating the
work of art (or material embodiment) from the essence of art
(statement D), and secondly by identifying the 'act' that creates
art with the reading or enjoyment of it (statement C). The first
step is equivalent to the doctrine that 'the true work of art is the
internal picture', in the mind either of its creator or of the
spectator or reader. This doctrine, it seems to me, owes its
plausibility to a confusion between the value and the existence
of works of art. That the value we attribute to a work of art
really belongs to its creator or to those who enjoy it is no doubt
true (though to say that the values that belong to creating and
to enjoying a given work of art are identical is quite another,
and far less plausible, story). On the other hand, only those
who have already adopted a very naïve mentalist philosophy
would claim that works of art *exist* only in the minds of those
who create or enjoy them. Works of art exist all right, in
galleries, books, musical-scores, etc., for us to go to them and
enjoy them: there is really no question about this. The relevant
question is whether such 'material embodiments' as the sounds
producible by a certain instrument, the effects to be got from a
certain pigment or stone, are relevant to the existence of what
we enjoy in—or from—works of art. Do these elements contribute to our enjoyment? It seems to me perfectly obvious that
they do: and from the side of the artist, the history of art contains
countless instances of how new materials, media, instruments,
etc., have determined both the direction and the vitality of
artistic inspiration.

   The first step in the required reduction, then, is, to say the least,
far from plausible. If it were justified, however, would the second
step follow? At first sight it might seem to; for artistic communication has somehow to be accounted for, and if the material
embodiments of art are inessential to it, it is hard to see what
artistic communication could consist in, unless in an identity of
creative 'act' and appreciative 'reading' or response. On the
other hand, Idealist æstheticians have to my knowledge nowhere

even tried to produce positive evidence in support of this second step; and, as will become clearer after an examination of statements (A) and (B) this is hardly surprising, since the proposed identification rests on a crude (though still common) misunderstanding of what is involved in reading or appreciating a work of art—or for that matter a single sentence or significant symbol.

We can now turn to statements (A) and (B), statements with which Idealist æsthetics makes its first contact with the facts of artistic creation and enjoyment. Both these statements are, of course, entailed by statement (C) which states their 'ideal identity'. We shall see, however, that they certainly state different things, different falsehoods, which require different logical and empirical considerations to expose their respective falsities.

At first sight statement (B)—that there is one act of Imagination that makes a particular work of art and gives it its individual meaning and value—seems simply one more instance of the bad philosophic practice of inventing unique 'acts' to correspond to, and account for, distinguishable 'mental products'—judgments, statements, arguments, plans, choices, and so on. In fairness to Idealist æstheticians, however, one must acquit them of the worst consequences of this common error, that of taking invented 'acts' as *actual*, of assuming that somehow, some day, they must be discoverable and describable, either directly, by improved introspective methods, or indirectly, on the evidence of causal inferences based on the supposition that they exist. Idealist æstheticians realize only too well that no empirical evidence could support the hypothesis of single acts as the necessary and sufficient causes of different works of art. The 'acts' they write of are *ideal*; attempts to describe them in experimental terms, to pin-point them in time or trace out their causal properties, would be utterly useless and misleading. Their 'ideal acts' answer simply to their conception of what is needed to account for the existence of different works of art, each having its own unique unity or wholeness. Quite obviously, Idealists insist, every successful work of art is a unity: therefore, on the principle that different fat oxen must be driven by different fat men, a distinct act of Spirit (acting in the grade or category of Art) is needed to account for every different work of art.

This conclusion presupposes that no alternative account of

the unity of works of art can be given. Now it is at this point that the empirical evidence, which Idealists brush aside so hastily, becomes relevant. It is no use, to be sure, to point out, as against the Idealist æsthetician, that a certain poem took a long time to write, that different parts of it were composed or suggested at different times, that fresh starts had to be made, false developments cut away, and so on. The Idealist will blithely subsume— or synthesize—any such ostensible variety and disjointedness in a piece of artistic creation under one of his ideal unity-ensuring 'acts'. What one must do is to use the empirical evidence— what artists have to tell us about their inspiration and methods of work—to suggest a framework of ideas which will account for the unity of at least *some* works of art, and do this much more convincingly than does the 'one act' theory of the Idealists. This, however, would be a major task in philosophical æsthetics; and all I can attempt, here, for the argument's sake, is the barest sketch of such an alternative theory, confining it, in the first instance, to the sort of unity we find in a good short poem. Among the tenets of this alternative theory would be: (i) The initial inspiration of a poem (for all that this may trail clouds of glory far back into the poet's past experience) is selected or recognized by him as the opening line (or core, or close) of a possible poem because of certain immediately striking features as values which it possesses. (ii) The extension or development of the poem can hardly be attributed to these same features, however; on the contrary, it will almost certainly be due to either (*a*) certain *other* features of the initial line or stanza which suggest, not its value, but its lack of value so long as it remains as it stands, *i.e.* incomplete, or (*b*) some further, relative independent 'inspiration', *i.e.* a line or stanza which was *not* in the poet's mind when he selected, or recognized the value of the 'initial inspiration' of his poem. (iii) The further 'organic' development of the poem is to be explained on similar lines: *i.e.* at different stages of the poem's growth different features of the lines or stanzas already formed suggest different developments. Then in (ii) above we saw how certain negative features or lacks in the 'initial inspiration' might call out the first extension of the poem. Later, when his work seems to the poet all but complete, some quite different negative feature of its opening lines may strike him, and suggest an appropriate ending for the poem. (iv) On this account there is no reason whatever why the poet, when he sees, say, this last relevant feature of his initial inspiration, should have clearly in mind—or should be able to revive in himself—those features in virtue of which he originally felt it as 'the beginning of a possible poem'. In other words, the poem's unity will not depend on some single, all-embracing act of the poet's imagination, but rather on the palpable incompleteness of the work at every stage—an incompleteness that keeps him at work until he has made of the poem as real a unity as his poetic capacity, his initial inspiration, the conventions of his literary form, and the genius of the language he uses, will allow.

I have sketched out my alternative to the 'one act' theory in terms of poetry, and of a poem that could be written by one man in one sustained creative effort. But it should be remembered—and this, I think, suggests an absolutely conclusive argument against the 'one act' theory—that much of the very greatest art is not of this kind at all—not the work of one sustained effort or of one man or even of one generation of men: for instance, some of the greatest works of architecture, works of many minds and many hands, which we nevertheless *do* admire as unities. Does the Idealist æsthetician seriously maintain that one act of imagination is responsible for, say, Cologne Cathedral? His knowledge of architecture must assure him that in such cases later developments and extensions are often of a kind that the original architect could not have imagined. The 'one act' theory of artistic creation simply collapses before facts such as these. On the other hand, the alternative theory sketched out in the preceding paragraphs can easily be adapted to take account of them. What could be more natural than to claim that late developments of a vast slowly-reared architectural work embody ideas suggested by the work as accomplished up to a given date—ideas coherent with, though not included in, the original design?

What of statement (A)? This at least, it may be felt, is an innocent enough statement. For, if there were not one way of reading, *e.g.*, a particular poem, how would objective criticism—say, how would the merest comparing of notes on artistic subjects—be possible? But, in spite of this argument, informed common sense will have its doubts. Is there only *one* way of 'reading', *e.g.*, *King Lear*, or Rembrandt's self-portraits? Certainly the history of literary and artistic criticism is full not only of reversals but of the most surprising developments in the appreciation of such masterpieces. (This accords with our natural feeling, in face of great works of art, that they contain much more than we have found in them.) But there is a much more powerful and general argument to be brought against statement (A). For the statement pretty clearly rests on the assumption that there is one way of reading every significant sentence or symbol, meaning by this that there is one 'thought' or 'inner experience' which every sentence or symbol must give rise to if it is properly understood. The fact is, on the other hand, that a sentence or any other significant symbol has meaning inasmuch as it can be interpreted in *any one* of an indefinite number of ways, logically connected to be sure, but emphatically not all contained or actualized in any single 'act' of understanding.[1] Two people no more need to have the same actual 'thoughts' in order to communicate information to each other than two people, *e.g.* a mother and her infant, need have the same 'thoughts' in order to communicate feelings of love to one another. For instance, two men read a road-sign marked 'TO OXFORD'. To the one, to judge by his immediate thoughts and actions, it means that he is on the right road and going the right direction, for Oxford is his goal. To the other it means he is on the wrong road, or at least going in the wrong direction, for his goal is Cambridge. Yet they have both read the sign aright, or, if you like, have understood it. But how can we, or can they, know this? Well, let us suppose that the sign is in fact wrongly directed: the two men then proceed in what are for them wrong directions and traverse weary miles, making useless minor corrections of their courses, till nightfall; and let us suppose that their circuitous wanderings bring them together again. Each tells the story of his misadventure, *wholly different at every stage from the other's*. But they both come back in their narratives to the road-sign, and at once each sees that this was the cause of his own, and of the other's, error. To generalize, the

---

[1] To have made this clear is, in my belief, one of the greatest achievements of modern philosophy. The above formulation is due to Peirce: other, to my mind, less adequate formulations are, (*a*) That the meaning of a sentence is equivalent to the sum of its consequences, and (*b*) That the meaning of a symbol can be shown only through its *uses*.

test of whether two people have read the *same* sentence or symbol
is always a kind of coherence test in respect of their subsequent
practice as well as a consistency test in respect of the language or
symbolic system to which the sentence in question belongs.

And now to apply all this to the reading of a picture or a
poem. Again two men look and read together. But the features
of the picture or poem that are emphatic to the one, that give
the lead to his interest, are regressive to, or utterly ignored by,
the other. (For proof, look at the different reviews of any original
work of art.) These initial differences, however, can be over-
come, or at least reduced, by patience, honesty, and good-will.
But the possibility that other differences will arise, on further
closer readings, can never be eliminated. And this points to an
all-important difference between the reading of works of art
and the reading of everyday information or history or science.
In the case of scientific sentences the context helps us to delimit
fairly rigorously the range of their relevant 'interpretants';
historical and ordinary informative sentences have a wider
fringe of possibly relevant interpretants, whose limits are much
harder to determine; sentences in poetry, or the arrangements of
objects in a picture or of notes in music, not only have a yet
wider fringe of interpretants, the very notion of 'interpretants'
has in these cases to be widened to include such things as the
relevant kind of association or the balancing chord or mass or line.
A full articulation of these differences should on the face of it
be one of the main tasks of philosophical æsthetics; but it is
obvious that Idealist æstheticians have neglected it entirely.

The Influence of Idealist Æsthetics. How, in view of their grave
logical defects, have Idealist theories of Art exercised so strong
an influence on literary and artistic criticism? In terms of statements (A) to (F) and our criticisms of them, we can now have an
answer, at least in outline.

Many errors in contemporary nineteenth-century criticisms
arc traceable to the tenets expressed in statements (E) and (F); for
instance, the doctrine that moral or religious considerations are
wholly irrelevant to all the arts, or its contrary, that they provide
the final canons in all; the doctrine that all art involves an element
akin to knowledge, or, again, its exact contrary; the doctrine

that all art is a form of craft, or, on the contrary, that the crafts, essentially, contain no artistic element. None of these sweeping assertions, attractive though they may be to bad critics whose great desire is to be done with thinking and be on to pontificate, can be maintained for a moment in face of what we actually find in the different arts, or even in different instances of what common sense brackets as 'one art'.. Thus, to take only literary examples, it seems clear that genuine religious feeling matters supremely to religious poets, but not to others; yet some writers are prized for their moral strength (*e.g.* Scott), while others are not (*e.g.* Byron); that in one novelist (*e.g.* Flaubert) the informative element is important, while in another it is slight (*e.g.* Hardy); that one writer certainly reminds us of a craftsman at work, whilst another seems 'but a wandering voice'. More important, however, are some of the beneficial effects traceable to these same essentialist tenets, for, to give Idealist æstheticians their due, these tenets do express, however misleadingly, a philosophical interest in problems arising from art and criticism. And this is more than can be said for those Naturalistic theories of art which have been the main rivals of Idealist theories for the past century: Taine's sociological theory of art, for instance, or Spencer's evolutionary theory, or Lombroso's, or Freud's psycho-pathological theories. These combine, really remarkably, the initial error of Idealist æsthetics (they assume that the word 'Art' stands for something common to all the arts) with a complete lack of interest in those problems that arise *exclusively* from the arts; and their effect can only have been to distract countless gullible readers from the arts themselves to their allegedly most important causes—soil and climate (with Taine), the needs of evolution (with Spencer), atrophied muscles (with Lombroso) and sexual repressions (with Freud). In the polemic against such theories as these the best Idealist æstheticians —Coleridge and Croce, for instance—stand up as lovers of art, and even as philosophers.

For somewhat similar reasons an educative value can be ascribed to statements (A) and (B). These at least have the merit of emphasizing as against Naturalistic theories, that, if we are to understand art at all, we must begin from what we see or read, or fail to see or read, in different works of art and from what seems to us to be said or done or intended by them. On the other hand, I find it hard to ascribe any value whatever to statements (c) and (d). The latter, which excludes the material embodiment of art from its essence, has served only to underwrite two dangerous tendencies which have pervaded criticism since the Romantic period. The first of these is the tendency of critics to discourse about their own feelings on, after, or before reading the work in front of them, instead of concentrating on the work itself; the second is the tendency to describe the (presumptive) impulse or motive of the artist rather than the job he has actually done. Statement (c), which identifies 'imaginative act' and appreciative 'reading', has had perhaps more baneful effects. For, if the plain man is told that there is one way of reading a poem and that this gives us its value, complete and perfect, he may feel some doubts. But when he is told that this one way of reading can be shown—on philosophical grounds, in particular on the ground that any *discussion* of the poem presupposes it—to be identical with the creative act that produced it, then he is likely to be cowed into silence. Idealist æstheticians have here proved themselves useful allies of arrogance and dogmatism in criticism, qualities that stand out unpleasantly in some of their own critical writings.

Alternative Methods in Æsthetics. What are the alternatives to Idealist and to Naturalist theories in æsthetics? There seem to me to be two important candidates for consideration, though to the best of my knowledge neither has anywhere been fully elaborated or even distinguished with a name. The first I shall call the attitude (rather than the theory) of informed scepticism. This scepticism, let it be emphasized at once, is confined to the possibility of worthwhileness of philosophical æsthetics—it is not scepticism about the worthwhileness or meaningfulness of criticism and valuation in the arts, still less is it part of a general sceptical philosophy. Its natural starting-point is the kind of criticism levelled in the previous section against statements (E) and (A). The informed sceptic will *deny* that the word 'Art', as commonly used, stands for any one thing, and will deny that for every given work of art there is one way of 'reading' that gives us its meaning and value. He will endorse what I have written above about the ill effects of these Idealist tenets on literary and artistic criticism, but he will push this line of attack much further. He will track down essentialist habits of thought in various departments of criticism, pointing out, for instance, the dangers of superficiality, if not of downright nonsense, in all discussion of 'the lyric', 'the drama', 'the concerto', etc. Unlike Idealist æstheticians, who make free play with analogies between the different arts, he will inveigh against the use of such phrases as the 'music of poetry', 'the logic of music', 'the poetry of colour', etc., reiterating such important platitudes as that when words do something that is described as 'musical' they can't possibly be doing what notes do; that although every piece of music has some structure and some have a peculiarly intelligible structure, this never bears a useful or illuminating resemblance to the structure of arguments; that, if certain colours thrill us as intensely as poetry does, the same is probably true of skating, high-speed motoring, and so on. In general, he will insist that every work of art is what it is and not another thing, and that, although a certain amount of comparison may assist critical judgment and appreciation, the job of criticism is not to show what is common to the work of art and all others—something that, if it existed at all, would be utterly trivial—but to show what is unique, and therefore important, in a given work.

The informed sceptic will also be on his guard against subtler forms of essentialist and dogmatic error in æsthetics. To give but one example: Croce has powerfully exposed the errors in criticism that result from a simple-minded acceptance of traditional artistic classification. To Croce's arguments on this score the informed sceptic will readily agree; but he will refuse to conclude from them, as Croce does, that the only difference between works of art is their respective artistic perfection (in Schleiermacher's phrase, *Volkommenheit der Kunst*); for this is simply another version of the essentialist tenet that Art *is* Imagination or the effective exercise of Imagination. On the contrary, the informed sceptic will insist that what is called 'the exercise of Imagination' is one thing in connexion with one subject-matter or material, another thing in connexion with a second. What is attempted and done in one novel, *e.g. Far from the Madding Crowd*, is not simply better—or worse—done than what is attempted in another, *e.g. Under the Greenwood Tree*. The 'exercises of Imagination' attempted in the two novels differ in kind; or, as we would more naturally say, the author tries to 'go deeper' in the former novel than in the latter. And on this ground the informed sceptic will endorse the common-sense conclusion that in the arts, as in moral life, level of aim counts for something—though, of course, not for everything: a fact which Croce, in this the most explicit of Idealist æstheticians, is forced to deny.

The informed sceptic, as I have presented him, may seem a thoroughly negative, even a pedantic, character: but in fact he is very far from being this. His scepticism and polemic are simply an attack on loose thinking in criticism in so far as this results from loose thinking in philosophic æsthetics; they are also a defence of freedom, individuality, freshness, uniqueness in the arts—the very things for which, in our age especially, the arts are most widely prized. As regard philosophical æsthetics, indeed, his attitude is entirely negative: he sees the philosopher's task simply as the correction and elimination of those philosophical errors, Idealist or Naturalistic, which have hitherto distorted serious criticism. But in other respects he is positive enough: he is the friend of serious criticism, and more, he is its gad-fly. He encourages criticism to stand on its own feet and have confidence in its own autonomous judgments and methods without looking for support to some showy philosophic scaffolding. He believes that whatever assistance Idealist æsthetics, for instance, have given to criticism could have been provided equally well, first, by a wide knowledge of the varieties and inter-connexions of the artistic traditions, styles, techniques, etc., and, secondly, by a closer examination of what is involved in reading, and in reaching agreement as to what can be read, in selected works of art.[1] This last proposal, we must emphasize, does not presuppose that there is only *one* way of reading every work of art or that there is something common to *what can be read* in any and every work of art. What the informed sceptic is proposing is not a supremely general inquiry of the kind that is naturally called *philosophical*; it is a continuous job for criticism itself— the attention which critics should always give to their own tools,

---

[1] Useful experimental data on this latter point can be found in Prof. I. A. Richards' *Practical Criticism*.

tools which have to be used in markedly different ways in different departments of criticism.

Is this position satisfactory? It seems to me to mark an advance, and an immense advance, in force, consistency, and practical usefulness, on any previous 'theories' of æsthetics. And I believe that any future 'philosophical æsthetics' must take most of the conclusions of informed scepticism as its starting-point. There are, however, two pretty obvious weaknesses in the informed sceptic's position. First, he admits that a certain amount of comparison between different works of art will help a critic in discussing their individual merits or failures; and here he leaves the matter, thinking no doubt that such comparisons must be of minor importance inasmuch as the critic's main concern is with the uniqueness, not the similarities, of different works of art. But we are surely entitled to ask: How much comparison is useful or justified in criticism, and comparison *within what limits*? Again—and this is perhaps the most important point—how *complete* must the analogy be between two works of art, or for that matter between two genres or schools of art, to be useful? Might not an analogy be extremely useful just because it works up to a point and beyond that point fails? Would it not, in such a case, help to bring out what is *unique* in each of the works compared?

The second weakness in the informed sceptic's position is this. He encourages criticism to examine its own methods, in particular to discover what is involved in reading, and in reaching agreement as to what can be read, in selected works of art. And he insists that this must be the job of criticism itself, since different methods, or devices or techniques, will assist to this end in different departments of art. But here again we are faced with the question of comparisons and of the limits within which useful comparisons can be drawn. And here, *prima facie*, there is a strong case for guiding our investigations by certain very broad analogies— *i.e.* analogies in respect of very general characteristics. Let it be granted that there is nothing important that is common to all our readings of different works of art; let us concentrate on the given work of art: still, is it not reasonable, in discussing how we read *this* work of art, to compare what we are doing with what we do in reading history or gossip or mathematics or natural science?

And on this issue philosophy, one would have thought, must have some useful advice to give.

These considerations point towards a second alternative method in æsthetics. It might be suggested that the job of philosophical æsthetics is to examine the main kinds of comparison and analogy found useful in criticism, with a view to determining as exactly as possible the points at which they cease to be illuminating and in fact give rise to contradictions or confusions. The informed sceptic would, however, retort that this proposal is pathetically optimistic and simple-minded. The kinds of comparison and analogy that criticism finds useful are probably as many and as various as the works of art criticism is faced with: certainly they do not fall into neat, tidy bundles. And even if the main kinds of comparison and analogy found useful in criticism could be arranged in bundles, little would be done to aid criticism: the critic himself, using his native powers of judgment, would still have to decide from which of them he must pull out the comparisons that will help to illuminate the work of art he is concerned with. What is proposed, in fine, seems little better than a card-index system for useful critical ideas.

In this retort the informed sceptic is undoubtedly right. Nevertheless, I am convinced that the suggestion just made points in the right direction: only, it is advanced wrong way on, so to speak. Could not the informed sceptic's objection be met as follows? I think he must grant that from time to time, in different departments of criticism, contradictions and confusions do arise just because a comparison or analogy, useful up to a point, is pushed too far. And he must agree, too, that some of these puzzles are peculiarly important, even though they may be relevant to only one tradition or school of art, or perhaps to the work of only one man or perhaps even to only one *work* of art. Why then do they count as important? I answer: only criticism can say why, but it is surely obvious that some lines of criticism, irrespective of their range of applicability, are peculiarly illuminating, and that some lines of criticism which *look like* becoming supremely important get bogged down in confusions of the kind just described. Now when this happens, is it not plausible to suggest that the philosopher, trained as he is to resolve logical puzzles, may be of assistance? When the suggestion is put in this way it no longer carries the implication that the puzzles of criticism can be sorted out and classified, and the philosopher can clarify them once for all. On the contrary, the natural assumption is that to every such puzzle that is resolved a hundred others will be waiting resolution. But this affords no reason for denying that such puzzles demand *philosophical* treatment. To argue in this way, indeed, smacks suspiciously of that last essentialist infirmity of philosophers—the demand that any method or technique they employ shall be universally applicable.

The alternative method I am proposing is, in the nature of the case, much more easily illustrated than described in general terms: for it is a 'journeyman's's[1] æsthetics, taking up work where work is to be done, whether at the explicit request of criticism or no. I shall therefore give one fairly detailed example of this method, and then suggest a handful of further problems it might be expected to solve. The problem selected is from literary criticism: no claim is made (to repeat) that it is relevant to all literature, or even to all poetry, or even to all English poetry of its period. Nevertheless, its importance seems to me unquestionable.

Illustrations of the Method Proposed. In his preface to the 1815 edition of his poems and in the *Essay Supplementary* of the same year Wordsworth discusses 'the creative or abstracting virtue of the imagination'. He notes shrewdly that the word 'Imagination' has been 'overstrained' and that 'poverty of language is the primary cause of the use we make of it', and he tries to remedy this situation by distinguishing what he calls 'different processes of Imagination'. His most interesting statements can be brought together under three heads. (1) In some poems the 'abstracting virtue' of imagination predominates, *i.e.* the poet abstracts from an object 'some of the properties which it actually possesses'; in other poems the 'creative virtue' predominates, *i.e.* the poet endows objects with 'properties that do not inhere in them, upon an incitement from properties and qualities the existence of which is inherent and obvious'. In either case the result is the important thing, *viz.* that the object 'is now enabled to re-act

---

[1] I take this phrase from Prof. Ayer. I do not know whether he would approve of the use I make of it.

upon the mind which hath performed the process, like a new existence'. (2) Wordsworth complicates the matter, however, by his more specific account of the *creative* processes of imagination. While emphasizing that these are in fact 'innumerable', he mentions in particular 'that of consolidating numbers into unity and separating unity into number—alternations proceeding from, and governed by, a sublime consciousness of the soul in her mighty and almost divine powers'. And he illustrates what he means by 'consolidating' and 'separating' by the passage in *Paradise Lost*, in which Satan is compared first to a fleet conceived (or seen) as an aggregate of separate ships and men, and then to a fleet conceived (or seen) as a unity. (3) Wordsworth's account is still further complicated by the following more general statement. 'When the Imagination frames a comparison, if it does not strike on the first presentation, a sense of the truth of the likeness, from the moment it is perceived, grows— and continues to grow—upon the mind; the resemblance depending less upon outline of form and feature than upon expression and effect, less upon casual and outstanding, than upon inherent and internal, properties. . . .'

The main difficulty involved in these statements can be brought out as follows. (*a*) In the statements under (1) Wordsworth clearly maintains that *both* processes of imagination, the creative and the abstracting, *alter* the object (so that it 're-acts upon the mind . . . like a new existence'). We might therefore be inclined to say: Imagination, as this far described, *falsifies* for the sake of a peculiar kind of pleasure. (*b*) Now this view would seem to apply most plausibly to the process Wordsworth calls 'creative'. But the illustration of this process given under (2) involves no falsification whatever. A fleet, from one standpoint (that of obeying one admiral, say), is a unity; from another standpoint it is a large number of ships and men; and both descriptions are true. The fact that Wordsworth's example is here not too happily chosen— that it illustrates the 'abstracting' process of imagination much more clearly than the 'creative' one—is here immaterial: what matters is, first, that the process of imagination described under (2) does not 'falsify', and second, that it is nevertheless chiefly to be prized for the gratification it affords to the mind performing it (see 'a sublime consciousness of the soul in her mighty and almost divine powers'). (c) When we came to the statement under (3) the reversal in Wordsworth's viewpoint is complete. The *truth* of the comparisons formed by imagination is now insisted on: but this 'truth' is still of a rather odd kind—a sense of it 'grows and continues to grow', and this fact about it now seems to be the main reason for prizing it.

How and why did Wordsworth get himself into this muddle? Why, first of all, does he talk about the *abstracting* virtue of imagination? Presumably, because in those poems which (through 'poverty of language') he calls 'Poems of Imagination', there is always a concentration on certain features of a 'real object' to the exclusion of others. Wordsworth describes this process in terms of his own poem *Resolution and Independence*. By a complex series of abstractions and comparisons we are presented with the figure of the old man 'in the most naked simplicity possible', so that when eventually he speaks it is indeed as if some embodiment of the most 'inherent and internal properties' of mankind were speaking. What Wordsworth calls 'the abstracting virtue' of imagination does stand, then, for certain easily recognized effects which we meet in certain poems. The basic issue is whether effects of this kind are more akin to arbitrary fiction and illusions or are more akin to the discovery of general, hitherto unsuspected, truths.

At this point we may usefully recall two contradictory philosophical positions with regard to abstraction. There is the well-known Idealist view that all abstraction falsifies; and there is the more ordinary view that abstraction is a process necessary for the attainment of much of our most certain knowledge, mathematical knowledge for instance. It is unnecessary here to articulate fully the latter view, or to explain fully how and why Idealists have misconceived the nature and uses of abstraction. Let us simply try to recall, in the homeliest terms, some of the reasons why abstraction is so fruitful a method in the mathematical sciences, why it helps us to see so many new truths. One obvious reason is that it allows us to concentrate on a limited class of properties, or, the other side of the same penny, that it frees us from the distraction of *other* properties which 'in reality' (in perceptual experience) upset the simplicity which mathematical reasoning requires. But the concentration which abstraction makes possible is not a fixed concentration—on a given figure, say: rather it is a concentration that enables us to pass rapidly over an immensely wide range of relations in which the figure, or certain parts or properties of it, might (and in some instances actually does) stand to other figures (or parts or properties of figures). This much is really obvious: though, needless to say, it isn't the whole philosophical story of the rôle of abstraction in mathematics. It is sufficient, however, for our present purpose— to illuminate Wordsworth's puzzle with regard to the 'abstracting virtue of the imagination'.

What he was trying to say, I think, was this. When a poet 'abstracts', what he succeeds in doing is to make us aware, in a manner somewhat analogous to the geometer's, of unsuspected relationships between an object he is describing and certain other objects. Looked at from this side his abstraction contributes to truth, to new general knowledge, even though the instance that gives rise to it be purely fictitious. On the other hand, there is one profound (and relevant) gap in this analogy. The abstractions of the geometer enable him to see and state with exactitude certain 'new' relationships of the figure or properties from which he begins; the abstractions of the poet enable him to do nothing like this, nor ought we to expect them to. The poet's abstractions strip the object from which he begins of 'casual and outstanding' properties, and they leave us—with what? With a hitherto unsuspected resemblance that may not strike us on the first presentation, as Wordsworth confesses, and which, when it does strike us, 'grows and continues to grow'. This resemblance is not, like the relationships which the geometer constructs or demonstrates, clear-cut and definable: on the contrary, its effect—the thing that matters in poetry—is to be measured by its wide suggestiveness, by the way it touches, or half touches off, ideas held 'in power'. In other words, a comparison that depends on 'the abstracting virtue of the imagination' makes us aware of the vast range of unexplored relations in which our initial object stands to others. In this way abstraction 'enlarges imagination'.

Our discussion of Wordsworth's problem can now be summed up in a few words. The relevant point about abstraction, as used in mathematics, say, is that in abstracting we seem at first to be simply omitting certain facts from consideration, and yet, as a result of this, we are enabled to see an immense number of further, and usually more general, facts. Up to a point the effects of abstraction in poetry are analogous. There is, however, the all-important difference, that while the 'new truths' gained by the geometer's abstractions are explicit, definable, and deducible, those gained by the poet's abstractions are inevitably vague and indefinite in their range. And that is a most important feature of them; indeed, it is responsible for the peculiar 'pleasure of the imagination' to which they give rise. This pleasure requires, first, that the comparisons framed by imagination shall be so *new* that the object they start from shall come to 're-act upon the mind . . . like a new existence', and second, that such comparisons shall not be too explicit: otherwise it would be impossible for a sense of their truth 'to grow—*and continue to grow*'.

This problem, chosen to illustrate the journeyman æsthetician's methods, is by no means the only one of its kind that arises from Wordsworth's great prefaces. Others arise from his contradictory statements regarding the 'general and operative' *truth* of poetry and the 'duty' of poetry 'to treat of things, not as they *are*, but as they *appear* . . . to the *senses* and the *passions*', and from his theory of 'poetic diction'. The problem chosen is, however, probably the most important of all these, and it has the advantage of suggesting two other closely related problems that arise from the criticism of literature and of the plastic arts: one of these is provided by the fact that critics habitually praise *concrete* details, illustrations, allusions, etc., in poetry or prose of a generally reflective tenor, and habitually condemn details, allusions, etc., that are *personal* or, at least, *subjective*; the other is provided by the idea of *abstraction* as used by Cézanne in his analysis and vindication of his own methods of painting. I would not wish to urge, however, that the problem I have dealt with occupies a central or pivotal position among æsthetic problems. Others, quite as crucial, arise from the attempt to clarify the notion of reading a single work of art and of establishing agreement or coherence as between different readings of it. (It is by this approach, I suspect, that the whole problem of the *units* of meaning and value in the different arts can best be examined.) But, in general, no suggested list of æsthetic problems could possibly be exhaustive, or for that matter representative: for no one can lay down in advance the lines along which criticism must go, or can foresee the kinds of difficulty critics may not run into. Finally, while I believe that the method employed above is typical of the kinds of method which journeyman æstheticians will find most useful, I don't want to dogmatize or to be interpreted too narrowly on this point. New and more penetrating philosophical methods, highly relevant to æsthetic problems, may be produced at any moment, and it is the duty of journeyman æstheticians to look out for these and apply them. Indeed, why should journeyman æstheticians deserve a hearing, if they do not bring to their problems the best logical tools available: if they cannot claim, in the words of the most philosophical of all great poets,

'Selber
Bringen schickliche Hände wir'.

CHAPTER III

THE DREARINESS OF ÆSTHETICS

By J. A. Passmore

BRITISH philosophers, with some few exceptions, pay little attention to æsthetics; it does not figure largely in MIND, nor is it considered a disgrace to a philosophy department when æsthetics forms no part of its curriculum. Can this lack of interest in a field so intensively cultivated in France, in Germany, in Italy, in the Americas, be set down, merely, to Philistinism? That is a conclusion not without its attractiveness; it is significant that æsthetics, when it is discussed, is so often condescended to as a poor relation of ethics. Discussions of ethics may begin as follows: 'Is it true that moral distinctions are matters of taste, as is so obviously the case with æsthetic distinctions?' There is here displayed a willingness, almost an eagerness, to accept the view that æsthetic judgments are subjective (and hence, by implication, not worth discussing, suitable only for proclamation) which contrasts oddly with the concern that morals should have some more secure foundation. Yet we might well think that the evidence told all the other way, that one knows exactly how to draw attention to the weaknesses of a cheap novelette but is puzzled how to explain exactly why sentimentality is morally evil, that one can learn to distinguish the good from the bad in Indian sculpture or Chinese poetry far more readily than one can detect the peculiar virtues of Indian or Chinese modes of life. At least, we must be struck by the casualness with which aesthetics is so often dismissed; and there is certainly behind that casualness something of the Philistine conviction that Art, decidedly in contrast with Morality, is a thing of no particular importance.

Yet Philistinism is not a sufficient explanation of the prevailing distaste for æsthetics; there are philosophers who take works of art seriously and yet who share this distaste. Nor is this attitude by any means incomprehensible, for if books on æsthetics do not quite take the prize for dreariness, at least they stand very high on the list. Not unnaturally, a certain suspicion comes to attach to the whole subject; can it be that there is something about the nature of æsthetics which makes it peculiarly unilluminating? This Mr. John Wisdom[1] has recently argued, and it will be convenient to begin by considering the force of his denunciation.

He distinguishes between dull and interesting ways of talking about art. First for dullness—'One may pick up a book on art and it be very dull. It is dull when it tries to give rules, canons, which will enable us to deduce whether a picture or a poem is good. It is dull when it tries to set out in general terms what makes a good picture good' (4.1). How can it be more interesting? Perhaps by telling stories about artists—'how one was very poor and kept a little dog and so on'. But this, as Mr. Wisdom rightly insists, is certainly not æsthetics; it is not even criticism. Then some people will find it illuminating if we talk about 'what beauty is, what sort of difference there is between two people when one praises a poem and the other says it's very poor'. But that, so Mr. Wisdom argues, is 'meta-æsthetics', not æsthetics.

This latter point puzzles me. In the first place, Mr. Wisdom's apposition 'what beauty is, what sort of difference there is between two people ...' makes a very large assumption, the assumption that talk about beauty is really talk about differences between people; this might be a conclusion to which 'meta-æsthetics' finally makes its way, but could scarcely serve as a general description of 'meta-æsthetics'. Secondly, the 'talk about people' wouldn't itself be 'meta-æsthetics'; it would simply be psychology. And finally, it seems very odd to call a discussion of 'what beauty is' meta-æsthetics; that would rather consist, one might imagine, in trying to describe what æsthetics is, in the manner of this article. 'What beauty is' is normally supposed to be the main theme of æsthetics itself—to be identical indeed with that general discussion of 'what makes a good picture good' which Mr. Wisdom has already dismissed to the Kingdom of Dullness. The fact remains, and this is what, I think, Mr. Wisdom means, that talk about æsthetics isn't itself æsthetics, any more than 'the philosophy of history' is history, and it could be interesting even when the conclusion which it sets out to demonstrate is that æsthetics itself is irretrievably dreary.

[1] In his contribution to the symposium *Things and Persons* (Proc. Aris. Soc., Supp. Vol. XXII).

Thirdly, says Mr. Wisdom, a book on art can be interesting when the critic 'helps one to a juster apprehension of the works he writes about'; in more detail, 'a good critic by his art brings out features of the art he writes about, or better, brings home the character of what he writes about, in such a way that one can feel and see, see and feel, that character much better than one did before' (4.2). Here then is the other side in Mr. Wisdom's antithesis; a dull book 'tries to set out in general terms what makes a good picture good'; an interesting one helps us to see more clearly the character of a particular work of art.

Two points now suggest themselves: the first, that Mr. Wisdom doesn't mind explaining in some detail what makes a good *criticism* good, and he presumably doesn't think that his remarks are unilluminating. Now, I suppose it could be the case that writing about what good works of art are like is unilluminating, whereas writing about what good criticism is like is illuminating; but the curious thing is that the sort of remark which Mr. Wisdom makes about good criticism is precisely the sort of remark which many of us would wish to make about good literature in general. Good literature, I should be quite happy to say, 'brings home the character of what (the author) writes about, in such a way that one can see and feel, feel and see, that character much better than one did before'; again, I should say that it is 'revealing, moving talk' which is 'not directed towards showing that a work (its subject) is good or bad' but 'towards showing it to us for what it is'—other properties, these, which Mr. Wisdom ascribes to good criticism. To put the matter differently, what Mr. Wisdom calls a good criticism seems to me to possess qualities which overlap with those possessed by a good work of literature. And it is not at all plausible to argue that the very same remarks which are so illuminating when applied to criticism cease to give off any light when they are applied to literature itself.

The second point is this: when we call æsthetics 'dull', we may mean either that it doesn't interest us or (what I take to be Mr. Wisdom's as it is certainly my own intention) that it fails to reveal with any sharpness the characteristics of its subject-matter. Now, it may just happen that Mr. Wisdom thinks that æsthetics is dull because he isn't interested in the general properties of works of art, but only in the character of particular works; he may wrongly believe that aesthetics is dull, in the only sense in which its dullness would be a weakness in it, merely because it doesn't do the kind of things he wishes to be done. *The Republic*, of course, discusses this very point: Socrates distinguishes between 'the lovers of sights and sounds' and 'true philosophers'; the former he says 'are incapable of seeing or admiring the nature of real beauty' (V.246). Socrates is scornful of 'the lovers of sights and sounds', but we all fall into this class as far as certain of our interests are concerned; we like travelling but abhor geography; contemplate flowers with pleasure but know nothing of botany; take a lively interest in the lives of our neighbours but none in Freud. And so we find the travel-book illuminating but the geography text dull; enjoy a country-walk with the man who can point out flowers to us, without being won over to an admiration for Linnæus; are amused by the expert gossip but bored by the psychologist. So we shouldn't be surprised that most people prefer literary criticism to æsthetics, or that Mr. Wisdom should turn out to agree with them. This will not show that æsthetics is 'dull', in the important sense of that word.

In the end, indeed, Mr. Wisdom somewhat relaxes his original severity. He grants that books on æsthetics may contain remarks 'which are general and still not valueless'. This happens 'when some value is temporarily undervalued or perhaps has always been undervalued'. And he gives an example: 'Clive Bell emphasized the importance of the formal features of a work of art by saying that beauty depends entirely upon these' (5).

This admission is certainly the thin edge of the wedge. For how does Mr. Wisdom *know* that 'formal features' have been undervalued? Surely, that he can know this implies that he has a general theory of 'values' and their *real* importance, so that he can be led to reflect: 'I had always thought that the subject was the valuable thing (what makes a good picture good), but now Clive Bell has led me to see that formal features are also important'. Of course, his general theory isn't, in a way, of any interest to him once he has it; he will find books dull which merely repeat what he knows already; the only interesting general remarks, to him, will be those which challenge in some way the views that he has so far held. But this isn't a vicious sort of dullness; just as it isn't an objection to elementary economics that an economist may be bored by it. If new general statements about art can be illuminating, then so can old ones be.[1]

Mr. Wisdom doesn't then succeed, I think, in consistently maintaining that books which make general remarks about art *must* be dull, in a vicious sense; at the same time, I am prepared to agree with him that most of them *are* dull; why this dreariness, if it is not inevitable? One good reason is suggested by Mr. Wisdom: 'When it comes to what makes a good picture good or a good poem good the whole plan is a failure and is apt to lead not to understanding and discriminating feeling for what is good, but to that rigid and dead reaction to recognized points sometimes found in dog fanciers and characteristic of the Pharisees' (4.1). Books on artistic 'goodness', to put the matter differently, often try to provide a substitute for individual judgment; they are dull for the same reason that books on scientific method are often dull; they set out to destroy spontaneity and speculation, and to substitute for them the application of a mechanical method. As Mr. Wisdom suggests, what misleads is that there are (more or less) mechanical methods for testing the goodness of arguments (although, even then, if we surrender our judgment to the rules we occasionally do quite silly things, as every teacher of logic knows). The æsthetician looks for a parallel method for testing the goodness of works of art ('follow my prescriptions and you *can't* go wrong'); the ethical theorist for a way of testing the goodness of conduct; the methodologist for a way of testing the goodness of beliefs. And this leads in every case to an emphasis upon 'externals', upon techniques or whatever else lends itself to mechanical calculation. Thus the school-child has to write an 'appreciation' of a poem; he looks up his guide to literature; there he finds some pleasantly definite statements about rhythm and rhyme and assonance and alliteration ('How skilfully the poet repeats the letter 'p' to represent the patter of the child's feet!'). Rules about the 'unities', rules about the couplet, about colour, about decoration, or about

---

[1] Mr. Wisdom's argument reminds us of a passage in Peacock's *Headlong Hall*:

'Mr. Gale: I distinguish the picturesque and the beautiful, and I add to them, in the laying out of grounds, a third and distinct character, which I call *unexpectedness*.

'Mr. Milestone: Pray, sir, by what name do you distinguish this character, when a person walks about the grounds for a second time?'

dominants—this is the sort of thing a great many people are looking for and the theorist often sets out to supply this particular market. The things that matter about works of art can't be set out so simply; and even if we were to discover certain general features of good works of art, it would probably be quite as hard to tell whether a particular work has these features as it would be to settle on the general principles themselves.

One distinction must here be insisted upon: that between 'technical' points and 'formal' points. Technical points can be settled rapidly, by the application of rules; a formal point can only be made with difficulty, after the closest scrutiny of the specific work of art. To take an example from literature: the question—is this a sonnet?—can be settled (with some marginal doubts) by counting lines and rhyme-patterns. And, of course, nothing follows, from the fact that it is a sonnet, about the æsthetic qualities of the poem; although conclusions can be drawn about the cleverness of the author. But the Aristotelian question (understood as Aristotle understood it)—has this work a beginning, a middle, and an end?—cannot be settled by any mechanical method; and this, the formal problem, is, I should say, an *æsthetic* question. There is, in the recognition of formal qualities, no 'rigid and dead reaction to recognized points': to discover the form involves a strenuous effort, an exploration of a work which is always sufficiently novel to make an æsthetic consideration something of an adventure.

A main source of confusion (and consequent dullness) in æsthetics arises out of the failure to make this contrast between the formal and the technical, or to make it at the right point. Thus L. A. Reid in his *Study of Æsthetics* describes 'technical' criticism in the following terms: 'It is the kind of criticism which, applied to painting, includes comment on composition, on the balancing of lines, planes and volumes, on tactual and colour values, on the expression of depth. In poetry this class of criticism is concerned with things like the disposition of vowel— and consonant—sounds or of assonance and rhyme and rhythm and metre. Music also has its own technical jargon' (p. 22). Formal and technical questions are here confused; what corresponds in painting to the discussion of metre in poetry (admittedly a technical question) is not the *formal* question—how the volumes in the painting are related—but rather the discussion of perspective or of brushwork, of the technical methods, that is, by which a painter displays to us a three-dimensional structure through the medium of a two-dimensional surface, a task which corresponds to that of the writer in presenting human feelings to us through the medium of words. Similarly, the 'jargon' of the musician is in part technical and in part a method of describing the formal structure of the music (the disentangling of themes, and the description of their vicissitudes). It is not always easy to decide whether a particular question is technical or formal; some traditional problems (for example, the nature of style) may turn out to break down into a technical and formal component.[1] But certainly if all formal questions are dismissed to the limbo of 'technique', æsthetics is left bombinating in a vacuum.

Thus there arises a sort of dullness which lies at the opposite extreme from marks-giving; it consists in saying nothing at all in the most pretentious possible way. 'In clouded majesty here Dullness shone,' as Pope put it. Or we may quote T. E. Hulme: 'A reviewer last week spoke of poetry as the means by which the soul soars to higher regions, and as a means of expression by which it became merged into a higher kind of reality. Well, that is the kind of statement I utterly detest. I want to speak of verse in a plain way as I would of pigs—that is the only honest way.'[2] To which, of course, one can expect the retort—'but poetry isn't pigs'. No more it is: and there are special reasons why it is easy to make the slide from poetry to metaphysics, and not so easy to found one's metaphysics on a pig. For one thing, the ontological status of a work of art may provoke the typical metaphysical qualms; for another thing, poetry is often *about* what one might call, for short, metaphysical feelings.[3] But, still, poetry is a particular kind of thing, with its own properties, and it is worth (like pigs) taking seriously for itself. Æsthetics fails to illuminate, often enough, because the æsthetician wants

[1] For a discussion of similar problems in music see D. F. Tovey, *The Integrity of Music.*
[2] T. E. Hulme, 'A Lecture in Modern Poetry,' printed in Michael Roberts, *T. E. Hulme,* Appendix II.
[3] For a recent, and particularly well worked-out, example of the transition from poetry to metaphysics see Prof. H. D. Lewis on 'Revelation and Art' (*Proc. Aris. Soc.,* Supp. Vol. XXIII), and for qualms about the status of works of art see Dr. Margaret Macdonald on 'What are the Distinctive Features of Arguments used in Art Criticism?' in the present volume.

to retain 'mystery' rather than to dispel it, to conceal his subject rather than to reveal it. He wants to treat art instrumentally, as a 'clue to reality'; his æsthetics is a spring-board to transcendental metaphysics. Consider, as illustration, the work of Jacques Maritain: 'The music of Lourié is an ontological music; in the Kierkegaardian style, one would also say "existential". It is born in the singular roots of being, the nearest possible juncture of the soul and the spirit, spoken of by St. Paul,' or again, 'Why should a musical work ever finish? . . . Let us say that as the time of the world shall one day emerge into an instant of eternity, so music should cease only by emerging into a silence of another order, filled with a substantial voice, where the soul for a moment tastes that time no longer is.'[1] Oh, for the *Journal of Agriculture* on pigs!

Woolliness of this sort seems to have a natural habitat in certain fields: in education, in sociology, in metaphysics, as well as in æsthetics. Why should these particular fields be thus distinguished by so fine an array of empty formulae? One reason, certainly, is that the metaphysician, the sociologist, the educationalist, attempt to reconcile oppositions in a formula so generally applicable, so empty of any intrinsic content, that everyone can interpret it to suit himself. Thus the sociologist engages in dull and pretentious talk about society's being 'an organic whole' when he wants to conceal the fact of social conflict; the educationalist talks about 'the ultimate welfare of the child and of society' as 'the aim of education' when he wants to make it appear that everybody expects the same kind of consequence from educational processes; the metaphysician, similarly, talks about 'cosmic purpose' or 'ultimate unity' in an effort to maintain that there is a single direction or pattern in the behaviour of things, a single end or purpose towards which everything works, in opposition to what seems to be the clear fact of the matter, that things work in very different ways, and move in very different directions.

---

[1] Maritain, *Art and Poetry*, pp. 97 and 83. Admittedly the translation of this work is in places incredibly bad. But it is interesting to note that reviewers took phrases like this description of Stravinsky's music—'shaken by tentatives, sometimes astonishing, of galvanization'—in their stride; so used are they to reading nonsense in books on æsthetics that even when the translator piled nonsense on nonsense they were unperturbed, to judge at least by their silence about the quality of the translation.

The woolliness of education, of sociology, of metaphysics, is understandable, then, as arising out of the attempt to impose a spurious unity on things, the spuriousness being reflected in the emptiness of the formulae in which that unity is described. We can easily understand the passions which lie behind this anxiety to reconcile. But why should the same sort of thing happen in æsthetics?

There are problems here which demand more attention than theorists have so far devoted to them; but the facts are sufficiently clear—whatever the reason, people do in fact become tremendously excited about æsthetic differences. Non-representational painting, for example, arouses in many people an extraordinary pitch of fury, quite comparable to the horror with which they contemplate atheism or communism; they display a desperate anxiety to maintain that what they like is æsthetically good (and, more passionately, that what they dislike is æsthetically bad), objectively good, that is, for they are not all inclined to the view that 'good' *means* 'liked by me'. Yet what they like is in fact such a hotchpotch of this and that, it being disreputable to condemn either Rembrandt or Sir Henry Leighton, or to praise either Cézanne or Salvatore Dali, that nothing but a high-sounding, empty formula can reconcile the irregularities of their æsthetic judgments. And the same applies, *mutatis mutandis*, to those who are affected by the desire to praise whatever is 'advanced'; sometimes, indeed, they share formulae ('sincerity', for example) with the bourgeoisie, for, as we said, the whole virtue of these formulae lies in the fact that they are infinitely accommodating.

. The serious student of the arts is in a rather different position: he will be prepared to admit that he enjoys detective stories without at all granting it as a conclusion that they must have aesthetic qualities; or he may say 'I can't bear to read war-books' without meaning by this that they are æsthetically bad. He may hang a painting on a wall because it is a painting by a friend, or of a friend, or because it reminds him of some familiar scene, while at the same time considering it to be of no importance as a work of art. It may still be true that he has not sufficiently distinguished within what he admires.

Let us consider the case of the literary critic. He will no doubt have realized that he sometimes likes what is trivial; he will not attempt to find properties peculiar to those literary works which he happens to like. But he may still try to find properties peculiar to whatever he *admires*, say to *Alice in Wonderland*, *Crime and Punishment* and *The Decline and Fall of the Roman Empire*. And then, I should say, he is forced either into woolliness, or into subjectivism (sometimes open, sometimes disguised), or into an emphasis on technicalities. For the properties to which we refer in describing the goodness of *Crime and Punishment* are conspicuously absent from *Alice in Wonderland*; and absent also (even if not so conspicuously) from *The Decline and Fall*.

No doubt there are resemblances between the three works; all three are written in words; all three have something to say about human beings. But still we judge them in quite different terms. It would not do for one of Dostoievsky's characters to disappear and leave only his scowl behind, nor for the Queen of Hearts to elaborate her motives; precisely what matters, to Dostoievsky, about Raskolnikov's crime is what would not matter, supposing Raskolnikov to be a figure of historical importance, to Gibbon.

Cannot we say that 'a good style', at least, is a general criterion? Only if that word suffers most peculiar mutations in meaning ('style is the choice and arrangement of words', 'the thought, that is the style too', 'the style, that is the man'), since, in any ordinary sense of the word, Dostoievsky has a bad style, and many inferior novelists a good one. The meanings arrived at by mutation, however, are so vague that 'style' no longer serves to discriminate at all. And if we are content to say of all three that they are 'works of genius' or 'the precious life-blood of a master-spirit', we are involved in a manifest circularity. ('The work is great because the man is great.' 'What is great about the man?' 'Why, his work!'); and we do not throw any light on the peculiar features of great works of literature.

What is needed, I suggest, is ruthlessness in making distinctions, a ruthlessness which will seem arbitrary only because the words we have to employ—'literature', 'good'—have an honorific sense. Thus my saying of *The Decline and Fall* that it is 'not literature' may be interpreted as a condemnation of that work, which is far from my intent. The works of Ethel M. Dell are literature;

the works of Gibbon are not. Accurately to distinguish between literature and other 'works in words' may be difficult (roughly, the literary work can be distinguished by its concern with human feelings as revealed in an incident); but it is sufficiently clear that we draw attention, in criticizing Miss Dell, to the absence in her work of properties we find in Shakespeare, not to the absence of the properties we detect in Newton, in Hume, or in Gibbon.

So far, nothing very revolutionary has been said. It amounts to this: if we define literature in a fashion as wide as that presumed in the ordinary 'histories of literature' we shall discover no distinctive properties (properties peculiar to 'good works of literature') in the works we take to be good. One can find confirmation of this view in the actual practice of 'historians of literature', as has recently been pointed out by René Wellek and Austin Warren in their *Theory of Literature*: 'In practice we get perfunctory and unexpert accounts of these authors, historians, etc., in terms of their speciality. Quite rightly, Hume cannot be judged except as a philosopher, Gibbon except as a historian . . .' (p. 10). When it comes to the point the critic is unable (except for some very general remarks about style) to talk about Gibbon in the terms he uses to discuss Shakespeare.

But even those who will grant that it is not merely arbitrary to deny that *The Decline and Fall* is literature, may boggle at my second contention: that *Alice in Wonderland* is not *good* literature. Once again, this should not be read as condemnation. *Alice* is charming, amusing, a better companion than Dostoievsky on a desert island, a work of genius, etc., etc. But *Alice* has not the properties possessed by *King Lear*, *The Brothers Karamazov*, *The Love Song of J. Alfred Prufrock*, *Ulysses*, the properties in terms of which we estimate the work of Mauriac, of Graham Greene, of Maxwell Anderson, of Jane Austen, of Priestley, and of Ethel M. Dell, properties regularly referred to by the ordinary critic of films, poetry, drama, and novel, properties which have clearly been in the mind of those literary theorists, from Aristotle on, who have not been content to lose themselves in mystification. If such properties are discoverable, and I think they are, it will not be merely arbitrary to describe as 'good literature' the works which possess these properties. There is no reason why we should not continue to admire works which we yet describe as 'bad literature'; the fact that they are not 'good literature' does not prevent them from being 'good thrillers', 'good ghost stories', 'good nonsense'.

Then when shall we want to argue? Are we simply proposing a different and highly eccentric way of using words? Very much more, for what we have said can be contested at a number of points, and not on questions of usage. It can be disputed whether, say, *J. Alfred Prufrock* has distinctive properties in common with the rest of the group and not possessed by works we should admit to be bad (the ordinary novelette); or, assuming the group suitable, it can be argued whether, say, *Murder in the Cathedral* or Mauriac's *Thérèse* possesses the properties in question. And this, I suggest, is exactly how we proceed in the everyday business of critical discussion. Admittedly, we do not usually formulate an explicit list of good books; but, still, if we pick up a book, and read it in the expectation of its being good literature, we judge its claims out of our experience of Shakespeare, the great novelists and great poets; and if we depart from common judgments about what is great (rejecting, say, *Wuthering Heights*) this will be because we take the work in question to be of the character of a novelette, and so not to possess the properties we believe we can detect in good literature.[1]

Of course, there is no novelty in the attempt to discriminate within 'literary works' between books which are to be judged in quite separate ways; and Mr. Carritt[2] has recently suggested that the attempt to make distinctions of this sort 'leads nowhere, although it has said many good things on the way'. I am arguing, on the contrary, that it alone can lead anywhere; and I should quote, as an example of the impasse at which we arrive if we try to avoid such distinctions, Mr. Carritt's own æsthetics, summed up in the phrases 'beauty lies in seeming, feeling makes it so'—

[1] A method of the sort I suggest has recently been employed by F. R. Leavis in his *The Great Tradition*. It is possible to dispute Mr. Leavis's thesis by maintaining, for example, that works to which he ascribes certain properties do not in fact possess these properties; or, again, by arguing that the properties to which he draws attention would make it impossible for him to distinguish good literature from good moral theory (I am not saying that these criticisms could be made out, but at least they would be relevant). Merely to accuse him of 'narrowness', or (as one particularly fatuous critic did) of ignoring the fact that we often read novels merely in the expectation of entertainment, is quite to miss the intent of his work.

[2] *A Calendar of British Taste*, Introd., p. xi.

conclusions, it seems to me, which are not æsthetics, but the rejection of æsthetics.

This is a remark which perhaps needs some elaboration, although it is not my present intention to discuss Mr. Carritt's work in any detail. Mr. Carritt lays down in the first sentence of his *Introduction to Æsthetics* what we might at first take to be a mere truism: 'The subject of æsthetic philosophy . . . is obviously æsthetic experience'. And he continues, 'Its presupposition, therefore, is that rational sensitive beings such as men have a set of experiences pretty clearly distinguishable from others'. This is unexceptionable, if all Mr. Carritt means is that there can't be æsthetics unless we can make æsthetic distinctions; but not at all obvious if it means that there must be a set of entities called 'æsthetic experiences'. And this latter is Mr. Carritt's interpretation. It then appears that the method of æsthetics is introspection and that 'to deny that an experience is æsthetic out of deference to an æsthetic theory, although careful introspection testifies to its æsthetic nature, would be to tamper with the data on which alone the theory could be founded' (p. 19). Here we meet once again the Cartesian assumption that there is an inner world of 'experiences', about whose nature we cannot be mistaken, provided only that we are reasonably careful in examining them. And, conjoined with this, the further assumption that these experiences carry their own labels with them, come to us neatly ticketed as æsthetic experiences, moral experiences, religious experiences. The outcome, as usual, is scepticism; we know our own experiences so thoroughly because they are ours, but we have no possible way of knowing other people's experiences. 'Even in extreme instances', writes Mr. Carritt, 'it is seldom possible to be sure of another's experience' (27). This is to put the matter too mildly; if anyone cares to say 'in the presence of that object, I have an æsthetic experience', we might say 'take another introspection', but if he takes it, and is of the same opinion still, that is the end of the matter; for us to pit our judgment against his would be absurd; to draw attention to weaknesses in the work he is contemplating would be to attempt, quite pointlessly, to rob him of an æsthetic experience which is rightly his.

It is my view that unless we can discover properties in good works of art which are not present in bad ones, we are inevitably led into this, or some comparable, species of scepticism; and, further, that if we try to include in our theory whatever works are for any reason accounted 'good', no such properties can be found. Just at what point distinctions ought to be made is, of course, the serious question; the proof, I should say, that a distinction lies here rather than there (for example, at the point I have elsewhere suggested,[1] between dream-works and exposure-works) is that a particular line of fracture gives rise to interesting generalizations. If it is true, as I have been suggesting, that no interesting generalizations (no generalizations which show us something about the distinctive properties of good literature) arise out of the study of 'literature' as the ordinary histories of literature define it; and that, on the other hand, there are interesting properties in such works as *The Brothers Karamazov*, *Macbeth*, *Tartuffe*, *The Love Song of J. Alfred Prufrock*, *Ulysses*, and other equally interesting but different properties in *Alice in Wonderland*, *Kubla Khan*, and *The Snow Maiden* then that is the only case that can be made out (and the only case that needs to be made out) in support of the distinction which I have proposed.

To try to avoid such distinctions is like trying to find characteristics common to science and to astrology, and peculiar to the pair of them as compared with other human activities. There are mechanical resemblances—both the astrologer and the scientist make calculations, for example—but these resemblances haven't the same theoretical interest as those which link physics with chemistry, and astrology with palmistry. The astrologer calls us arbitrary if we generalize about science in such a way as to exclude astrology from its ambit; and many people will be indignant if we talk about literature in such a way that *The Decline and Fall* or *Alice in Wonderland* do not have the properties we ascribe to 'good' literature. But this indignation misses the point at issue: the possibility of discovering general and distinctive properties must determine our field.

Now, even if there are things which are worth saying about 'literature' (in the sense in which we have defined it), and other things which are worth saying about music, about architecture, and so on, it still does not follow that there is such a thing as

[1] 'Psycho-Analysis and Æsthetics' (*Aust. Jnl. of Psych. and Phil.*, Sept. 1936).

æsthetics, in distinction from literary theory, musical theory, etc.; it seems to me possible at least that the dullness of æsthetics arises from the attempt to construct a subject where there isn't one. The alternatives have commonly been posed as if we had to say either that there is æsthetics or else that 'it's all a matter of personal preference', but perhaps the truth is that there is no æsthetics and yet there are principles of literary criticism, principles of musical criticism, etc. We have no real difficulty in saying what is wrong with a cheap novelette, or what is wrong with the Albert Memorial, and we can do both of these things without being dull: the dullness arises if we try to develop a general theory of 'wrongness' in art.

But surely, it may be replied, we speak of any form of art as 'beautiful' or 'ugly'—must there not be general properties which these descriptions convey? I should suggest, on the contrary, that there is something suspect ('phony') about 'beauty'. Artists seem to get along quite well without it: it is the café-haunters, the preachers, the metaphysicians, and the calendar-makers who talk of beauty. We wouldn't feel quite comfortable if we called the etchings of Goya or the engravings of Hogarth beautiful; nor would we naturally employ that word as a description of Joyce's *Ulysses* or of Moussorgsky's *Boris Goudonov*. 'Beauty' is always nice, always soothing; it is what the bourgeoisie pays the artist for; it is truth as compared with facts, goodness as compared with spontaneous creative action. In more professional circles, it is the refuge of the metaphysician finding a home for art in his harmonious universe, attempting to subdue its ferocity, its revelations of deep-seated conflict, its uncompromising disinterestedness, by ascribing to it a 'Beauty' somehow akin to goodness.

When Lessing in his *Laocöon* (Ch. 2) objects to the work of Pyreicus 'who painted, with all the diligence of a Dutch artist, nothing but barbers' shops, filthy factories, donkeys, and cabbages, as if that kind of thing had so much charm in Nature and were so rarely seen', when he demands (Ch. 24) that painting should 'confine herself solely to those visible objects which awaken agreeable sensations' or that 'one should not force expression beyond the bounds of art, but rather subject it to the first law of art, the law of Beauty' (Ch. 2), he has usage on his side.

'Why, when there is so much beauty in the world, does the artist want to paint ugly women, or the novelist depict sordid scenes?'—that is the regular complaint of the Philistine. 'Beauty,' in this sense, is clearly relative to social conventions and individual disgusts; we may attempt to purge the word for the purposes of æsthetics, but certainly we shall be cutting across the grain of usage.[1] The subjectivists are probably right about beauty; but no consequences follow of any importance for æsthetics.

At least, though, we must allow talk about *good* literature, *good* architecture? 'That's really good' is the typical remark of artists and of critics. And it is applied equally to literature and to music, to painting, and to architecture. There's another phrase, often substituted: 'he's really brought that off'; this, I suggest, is what goodness means—'bringing it off'—accomplishing his special task. And in literature this involves something quite different from what it involves in painting; the link between the two sorts of 'goodness' is no closer than that between a good painting and a good theory, or between a good piece of business and a good shot at tennis. It is good because it is well done, but there is no sort of 'well-doing' peculiar to art, although there is a sort of well-doing peculiar to each specific art.[2]

The remarks of artists are, of course, often of technical rather than æsthetic interest; 'he's done a good job' may mean 'he has solved a ticklish technical problem'. Unless we insist, again, on the difference between technical and formal considerations, we may be bewildered by the apparent diversity of judgments about 'goodness'; one painter, for example, is praised for the clarity of his colours, and another because the objects on his canvas shade almost imperceptibly into one another. These are not, however, contradictory æsthetic criteria. We are in either case admiring the skill of the painter, but the æsthetic question remains: the

[1] Miss Helen Knight in her *The Use of 'Good' in Æsthetic Judgments* (an article which I came upon late in the composition of this article, but with which I should agree on a great many points) suggests that 'on the whole we commend the works of man for their goodness, and the works of nature for their beauty'. Perhaps beauty has a stricter sense in the description of landscape than in any other context and could be reserved as a description of the 'natural'. Even then, however, it would need to be purged of its usual connotations; for beautiful landscape is not always 'agreeable' or 'nice'. [*Ed.* See Miss Knight's essay in this volume, pp. 147–60.]

[2] Here, especially, I find that Miss Knight has anticipated my conclusions. But I should hope to avoid the fragmentation of criteria which she takes to be inevitable.

question, that is, of the formal relationships between the three-dimensional objects thus depicted. These relations may sometimes be best conveyed by clear lines, sometimes by fuzzy ones. Similarly, what is a bad style in one context is a good one in another. The turgid rhetoric in which King Claudius explains his conduct to the Danish court is, in that context, precisely right; we condemn Lyly's characters because they speak euphuistically, whatever the occasion, but it would be absurd to object to Osric on the same ground.

We have here distinguished a technical from an æsthetic use of 'good'. How can this be done if there are no æsthetic properties? A good detective story need not be a good work of art; people who 'like to curl up with a good book' aren't passing æsthetic judgments. It is therefore impossible to define 'the æsthetic use of "good"' as 'the use of "good" in which it is applied to works of art', for we can rightly describe a work as 'good' without ascribing æsthetic characters to it. The solution, I think, is that although there are not 'æsthetic properties' common to all good works of art, there is what we may call an æsthetic approach to works of art, just as there is a scientific way of considering a thing, without it being the case that things have scientific characters; or again, there are not technical properties but there is a technical approach. The technical approach raises the question: 'how was this work put together?'; the historical approach: 'when was it done, influenced by what?'; the bio-graphical approach: 'what does it amount to, as an event in its creator's life?'; the æsthetic approach: 'how does this work hang together?'. But 'hanging together'—or, to use more genteel expressions, coherence, harmony, integrity, form—is not a special æsthetic property, recognizably the same in various works of art; it is more like a category than a property, suggesting the kinds of question which are to be asked rather than the sort of property that is to be looked for. We only arrive at the level of properties when we ask specific questions about specific works.

This doctrine, that we must seek different properties in different art-forms is not, of course, a new one; Croce attacks it in his *Essence of Æsthetic*.[1] But Croce very much confuses the

[1] As translated by Douglas Ainslie, p. 53.

issue by attacking two quite distinct 'prejudices' at the same time; the first, the doctrine of literary kinds (tragedy, comedy, pastoral, epic, etc.), the second, the doctrine of æsthetic kinds (painting, music, literature, etc.). To the first one can certainly object, as Croce does, that the boundaries between, say, tragedy and comedy can never be fixed with any precision, but do we ever find ourselves in doubt whether we are confronted by a symphony or by a statue?

What Croce would have us believe is that whether we are contemplating architectural masses, or a Bach fugue, or a play by Shakespeare, or the paintings of Cézanne, what we are in every case *really* contemplating is a certain form of human feeling. This is a particular variety of æsthetics now widely accepted. Whether the feelings we then admire are supposed to be those of the artist, or whether we admire our own feelings anthropomorphically ascribed to inanimate objects—'we transform the inert masses of a building into so many limbs of a living body, a body experiencing inner strains which we transport back into ourselves'[1]—the suggestion is in either case the same, that nothing inanimate can have æsthetic properties in itself, that nothing is 'beautiful' except the human spirit. Art then most eminently plays a metaphysical role: it stands for the animistic as against the scientific view of things, showing what things 'mean' as distinct from what they are. Whatever describes the work itself is dismissed as 'technical'; æsthetics is no longer particularly concerned with works of art.

Such a theory, however, can never show that a work 'means' one thing rather than another; for what a work 'means' will depend upon what it suggests to a particular observer. (And there is nothing here to correspond to the rules of linguistic usage; to call architecture a 'language' in the hope of thus avoiding arbitrariness is to pretend there is a convention where none in fact exists; nor should we seek to establish one.) Mr. Carritt's scepticism is the only honest conclusion of all such doctrines. That the *Pastoral Symphony* is more fully expressive of cheerfulness than *Pop Goes the Weasel* or that Durham Cathedral is more

[1] Lotze, *Microcosmos* (Bk. V, Ch. 2) as quoted in Vernon Lee's *Anthropomorphic Æsthetics* (in her *Beauty and Ugliness*, p. 18). See for a critical examination of 'expressionism', John Anderson, *Some Questions in Æsthetics*.

expressive of religious feelings than the Methodist Chapel at Llangollen—these are matters regarding which argument would be absurd; it is as if, to take a strictly comparable case, one person were to argue that Monday is a yellow day and another that it is a red day. Concerning such merely personal associations there can certainly be no dispute. Meanwhile people go ahead with their ordinary æsthetic discussions, criticizing literature as literature, music as music; asking what the work of art *is*, not what it 'means', quite as if they were concerned here, as in science, with particular matters of fact. And if this were not so, criticism, education, controversy, would be impossible.

To return to our main theme, there is no way of *proving* that good works of art have no distinctive properties in common (properties, that is, which are not to be found also in bad works of art or in whatever is well done, whether a work of art or not). One can only draw attention to what happens when æstheticians try to nominate such properties. Sometimes the æsthetician substitutes for æsthetics something quite different; for example, the theory of art. For certainly art (good and bad) may be considered as a social institution; we can ask how it arises, what social effects it has, under what conditions it flourishes; there is a phenomenon, art, which can be studied socially, psychologically, or ethically. Or else, and very commonly, he substitutes metaphysics for æsthetics; or, on the other side, the study of techniques. Sometimes the characteristics which the æsthetician mentions—unity, structure, integrity—are general categories rather than anything at all peculiar to works of art; here, we have suggested, the æsthetician may unwittingly be on the right track, but certainly he has mentioned no æsthetic properties. And sometimes (this also can be illuminating) he stretches modes of criticism which are applicable enough in a particular art in the attempt to make them cover every art. Thus, if it be said that good works of art 'develop a theme', we know what this means in music, we may feel that we can make some sense of the phrase in criticizing literature (although already, I suggest, we really mean something quite different), but how could we possibly apply this critical method to sculpture? Similarly, 'balance' may have a specific meaning in the plastic arts, but can it be non-metaphorically applied to literature and to music? And more often than not, the æsthetician does none of these things; he simply talks dreary and pretentious nonsense. The alternative, I suggest, isn't subjectivism but an intensive special study of the separate arts, carried out with no undue respect for anyone's 'æsthetic experiences', but much respect for real differences between the works of art themselves. In this sense—art for art's sake!

CHAPTER IV

FEELINGS

By Gilbert Ryle

WE talk of ourselves and other people 'feeling' things very multifariously.

1. There is the perceptual use, in which we say that someone felt how hot the water was or felt the rope round his neck or felt that the spoon was sticky. Feeling, in this use, is one of our ways of detecting or discerning things. We feel with our fingers or our tongues, as we see with our eyes, and we can be good or bad at detecting different sorts of things in this way and we can improve or deteriorate at it. We can try to feel things and either fail or succeed, and we can feel things indistinctly or distinctly.

If my teeth were chattering, I might detect the fact by hearing them or by seeing them in a mirror. Or I might feel them chattering with my tongue or lips. But ordinarily I feel them chattering without using instruments, fingers, tongue, or lips; just as while I might find out that my feet were cold with my hand or with a thermometer, ordinarily I find it out without employing either instruments or other bodily organs. Should I say that I feel that they are cold in or with my feet themselves? In real life I do not say this. I just say that I feel that they are cold. But if my feet were very numb, and I were asked whether they were cold, I might have to reply 'Wait a minute. I must feel them with my hands, since, for the moment, I cannot feel whether they are warm or cold in or with my feet themselves'. The fact that I do not know which preposition 'in' or 'with' we should use to make this contrast, shows how unnatural the usage is.

2. Connected with the perceptual use of the verb 'to feel', there is its explanatory use. I feel for the matches in my pocket or feel my horse's legs. This explanatory use of the verb stands to its perceptual use as 'peer' and 'look' stand to 'see' and as 'listen' stands to 'hear'. Feeling, in this use, can be successful or

56

unsuccessful and can be continued for a period, intermitted and resumed. It can be careful, skilful, and methodical, or haphazard and unsystematic. A doctor may carefully feel my pulse, yet fail to feel it, just as he may peer but fail to see.

3. Also connected with the perceptual use of the verb, there is what I may call the mock-use of it. The condemned man already 'feels' the rope round his neck, though there is not yet any rope round his neck, just as he 'hears' the tolling bell, though it is not yet tolling, and he 'sees' the gallows, though they are not yet erected. Sometimes we say 'feels as if', 'seems to feel', or 'imagines he feels', to avoid having to produce the ironical tone of voice or the quotation marks which indicate the mock-use of the verb. (All words are capable of mock-use. 'Your "lion" was only a donkey' is not a self-contradiction.)

4. Different from any of these is the use of 'feel' in connection with such complements as aches, tickles, and other local or pervasive discomforts. To feel a tickle and to have a tickle seem to be the same thing. The spoon may be sticky or my teeth may be chattering, without my feeling it (or seeing or hearing it). But there could not be an unfelt tickle. And whereas, if numbed, I might only indistinctly feel my teeth chattering, there is no question of indistinctness or distinctness in my feeling a tickle, but only, what is quite different, a question of the tickle being violent or faint, or, which is different again, a question of the tickle having much, little, or no attention paid to it. In this use of 'feel', one cannot try to feel an ache or tickle, and one cannot be or become good or bad at feeling such things. Feeling, in this sense of having, is not a sort of discerning, detecting, or finding, or, of course, any sort of searching or rummaging. Pick-pockets may become adept at feeling coins and watches in other people's pockets. No one can be good or bad at feeling itches.

Conversely, while we are ready to classify the tickle or ache that one has as a special sort of feeling or sensation, we certainly will not classify as a special sort of feeling or sensation what one feels, in the perceptual use of the verb. What one feels, in the perceptual use, is the heat of the bath water or the chattering of one's teeth, or a watch in someone's pocket.

5. Quite different, again, is the use of the verb 'feel' when

followed by an adjective of what I shall vaguely call 'general condition'; for example, 'to feel sleepy, ill, wide awake, slack, fidgety, vigorous, startled, uneasy, depressed, cross', and so on. There is no sharp line between the general conditions which one would call 'bodily' and the general conditions which one would call 'mental'. One would report feeling out of sorts to a doctor and report feeling depressed, perhaps, to a psychiatrist. But both practitioners might be interested to hear that one felt languid, fidgety, or vigorous. Startling world news might stop one feeling sleepy, while something out of a bottle might dispel one's depression. No argument is needed to show that this use of the verb is not its perceptual use or its exploratory or its mock-perceptual use.

On the other hand there is a strong tendency to assimilate it to the use of 'feel' in 'feel a tickle'. As a certain sort of distressing feeling or sensation is *had*, when one has a tickle; so it is often supposed, there must be some feeling or sensation, perhaps of a rarified or complex kind, which is had by a person who feels unfit or wide awake or anxious. But the trouble is that for any specific feeling that can be mentioned as capable of being had, it is always possible for a person to say that he feels unfit, wide awake, or anxious though he has not got that specific sensation. Certainly when I am anxious, I often do have a sort of heavy and coldly burning sensation in the pit of my stomach. But I should never say 'Oh no, I don't feel at all anxious, for I have not had that sensation in the pit of my stomach once to-day'. Or I may feel angry and not have the tense feeling in my jaw muscles or the hot feeling in my neck, even though very often I do have these or other sensations when I am angry.

Conversely, for any such specific feeling that you like to mention, it is possible for a person to have that sensation and not to feel unfit, say, or depressed or angry. The tense feeling in my jaw might go with cracking nuts or watching a trapeze artist, and the hot feeling in my neck might go with standing on my head or holding my breath. So there is at least a *prima facie* case for the view that to feel out of sorts or vigorous or sorry does not entail that any specifiable feelings are had, in the way in which aches are had.

There is one important difference inside this use of 'feel'. If I feel unfit or tired or worried or cross, I can always significantly and sometimes truthfully say that I feel *acutely* or *intensely* so. But if I feel fit or fresh or tranquil or good-tempered, there is no question of my condition being intense or acute. But here I can say instead that I feel *completely* well or *perfectly* contented, as I cannot say that I feel completely cross or perfectly worried. The point is this. Just as when I say 'I met nobody', I am not reporting a meeting, but the absence of one, so when I say 'I felt absolutely calm or perfectly at my ease or quite well' I am not reporting that I was upset in any way, but that I was not upset at all. Epistemologists sometimes talk of the feelings of familiarity and sureness. Now I can feel acutely strange or faintly dubious. But when I do not feel at all strange or dubious, then to say 'I felt quite at home or confident' is just to say that I did not feel at all strange or dubious. Our word 'sure' derives from the Latin *securus*, '*free* from anxiety'.

6. There is the very common usage in which we speak of feeling that something is the case. I can feel that there is a flaw in your argument, or that a thunderstorm is brewing, or that she has something on her mind. If someone feels that something is the case, he does not *think* that it is the case. He is inclined to think so, but has not yet taken sides. It is like the difference between mistrust and accusation.

If a person thinks that something is the case, which is not so, then he is in error. But if he merely feels that something is the case, which is not so, then, though he is attracted by error, he is not wedded to it. He is tempted to hold a certain view, but he has not yet succumbed to the temptation. His mind is not yet closed; it is still ajar. This use of 'feel' is obviously not the perceptual, the mock-perceptual, or the exploratory use. But nor does it seem to have much to do with the use in which people say that they feel aches and therefore have more or less distressing feelings or sensations. For no special sensation is had when I feel that there is a flaw in your argument. The questions 'Where do you feel it? Would an aspirin allay it? Have you got it now? Does it come and go, or is it there all the time?' are not pertinent questions. My feeling that there is a flaw in your argument can be strong, but not intense or acute, continuous or intermittent. I am in no distress. (The edges of the distinction between 'feel

E

that' and 'think that' are not hard. Feeling that something is the case slides into thinking that it is the case; and we often use 'feel that' instead of 'think' as a sort of polite hypocrisy.)

7. Lastly, there is an interesting idiom, which I daresay is a purely English idiom, in which we speak of feeling like doing something. I may say that during the funeral service I felt like laughing, or that in the train I felt like taking a nap. It is a near-paraphrase of this idiom to say that I was tempted to laugh or to take a nap; but it does not always do. For we speak of temptation only when there exists some scruple against yielding to it. Thus I was tempted to laugh at the funeral, in a way in which I was not tempted to take a nap in the train, since there was no objection to my sleeping. Perhaps a garrulous neighbour kept me awake, but scruples did not do so. There is, however, a special point about feeling like doing something. If the clown at the circus says or does something funny, I laugh straightaway, and I do not then say that I had felt like laughing. I reserve the expression 'I felt like laughing' for occasions in which I was inclined to laugh, but was, at least for a short period, inhibited or prohibited from doing so. It is only when there has been time for the idea of doing something to occur to me, and to occur seductively, that I want to say in retrospect that I felt like doing it. It is when the action to which one is inclined is delayed or impeded or prevented or when its consummation is relatively slow or only partial that one wants to speak of having felt like doing it. My toes tingle to kick the intruder downstairs only when I do not instantaneously do so. I feel like having a smoke only when I am not smoking.

Here again, there seems to be little connexion between feeling like doing something and having a sensation. A man may feel like writing a letter to *The Times* protesting at the unfair incidence of Death Duties; but we do not think that there is a peculiar feeling (or covey of feelings) associated with writing to *The Times* on this subject; and if there were, we should not know what sort of feeling this was, since we have never done the thing. So the fact that we understand perfectly what is meant when a man tells us that he felt like writing such a letter to *The Times*, shows that we do not construe his statement as a description of some special feelings that he has had.

On the other hand, there is an important connexion between, for example, feeling tired and feeling like sitting down, or between feeling indignant and feeling like writing a protesting letter to *The Times*. That he should, from time to time, feel like doing certain sorts of concrete things is one of the things that we expect of a person who is in this or that mood or general condition. He is in the mood, *inter alia*, to have such ideas not only occur to him but occur seductively. We expect the angry person not only to talk gruffly, scowl, and slam the door, but also to entertain fancies of doing all sorts of hostile things—most of which, of course, he cannot do and would not permit himself to do, even if he could.

.   .   .   .

Here, then, are seven different uses of the verb 'to feel'. I expect there are plenty more. I have, for instance, said nothing of feeling pleased, soothed, relieved, triumphant or exhilarated. But seven are enough. Consideration of them is liable to set up in us two opposing theoretical tendencies. To begin with, we have a strong craving to assimilate all the other uses to one of them. Perhaps in emulation of chemists, we hanker to reduce to a minimum the number of kinds of elements or constituents of which minds are made, and accordingly we hanker to make the word 'feeling' stand for a homogeneous something. Legends about the soul being tripartite foment (and sometimes derive from) this emulation.

We are like the child who cannot help supposing that all the MacTavishes in the world must belong to the family of Mac-Tavishes who live next door. It is a family surname, isn't it? So it must be the name of a family. When subject to this craving, we are particularly liable to assimilate all the uses of 'feel' to its use in 'feel a pain or tickle'. Or sometimes we try to assimilate even feeling pains and tickles to that perceptual use in which we feel certain anatomically internal things like palpitations, cramps and creakings in the joints. But later, when we have attended to even a few of the grosser differences that there are between, for example, feeling for a box of matches and feeling that there is a flaw in an argument, or between feeling homesick and feeling a shooting pain in one's right eye, we tend to suppose that it is a chapter of sheer linguistic accidents that the one verb

'feel' is used in all these disparate ways; and that English would
have been a better language if it had provided seven (or more)
quite different verbs. Having realized that not all MacTavishes
need be members of the family next door, we incline to scout
the idea that there might even be a common clan-origin for
them, and to reproach Somerset House for permitting people
from different families to have the same surname. In resistance
to both of these two tendencies, I now want to suggest that
though the seven cited uses of 'feel' are not members of one
family, still they do have some traceable genealogical connexions.

   In discussing the perceptual use of 'feel', I pointed out that
when I detect my teeth chattering, this detection need not take
the form of seeing or hearing or feeling with finger, tongue or
lips. That they are chattering might be perceived, to use the
unnatural expressions, in or with the teeth themselves. With
some anatomically internal things, this is even more conspicuous.
If one of my joints creaks, neither you nor I may be able to
hear or feel the creaking with our fingers. But I (unless anæs-
thetized) can do what you cannot; for I can feel it creaking in
or with the joint itself. So I can perceive some things that you
could not easily, if at all, perceive in any way, unless perhaps
you had me on the operating table. For my knee joint is mine
and not yours, so you cannot feel things in it, as I can do. Compare the following cases. When I frown slightly you are, usually,
in a much better position than I for detecting it, since you can
see it, while I cannot see it or, ordinarily, feel it. When my right
fist clenches, you are in only a slightly worse position than I,
for we can both see it, and we can both feel it, you with any of
your fingers, and I with the fingers of my left hand. But besides
this, I can also, unless numbed or recently hit on the right funny
bone, feel it clenched in my right fist itself. But when my throat
is constricted or my heart thumps you are in a very much worse
position than I, for you can detect this only if you take rather
elaborate steps; whereas I can detect it without taking any steps
at all. So for some (not all) such facts about my body, you may
find it highly convenient and sometimes quite necessary to ask
me what I feel. We have here a sort of (graduatedly) privileged
access to such things as palpitations of the heart, cramps, and
creaks in the joints.

If a cobweb brushes my cheek, I may or may not detect it; but if I do detect it, I may detect it not by sight, but by feeling it in the cheek that is brushed. But, further, if a cobweb brushes my cheek, I may feel a tickle, and as we have seen, feeling or having a tickle is not the same sort of thing as distinctly or indistinctly perceiving something brushing my cheek. It would be just a poor joke to say that I have felt two things; namely, something brushing my cheek, and also a tickle. I have a tickle, perhaps, *because* something lightly brushed my cheek; but this could be the case without my having detected anything brushing my cheek.

Now the place that I want to rub or scratch is the part of the cheek that the cobweb brushed; and the part of the cheek that the cobweb brushed, is, if I detected it in this way at all, the part of the cheek in which I felt it brushing me. In this sort of case I find where to scratch *pari passu* with finding where something brushed me; and this I may detect with the part of me that is brushed. The transition from saying 'I felt something brush my cheek' to saying 'I felt something tickling my cheek' and from there to 'I felt a tickle on my cheek' is an easy and natural one. But it certainly is a transition. The adverbs 'clearly' and 'distinctly' can qualify the verb in its first use, but not in its third use. The second use, 'I felt something tickling my cheek', is a bridge between the two.

What sort of a thing is a tickle?, or rather, what sort of a state of affairs am I reporting when I say that I have or feel a tickle? It is all right, but it gets us no further, to say that a tickle is a 'sensation'. It actually impedes progress, if we recall what the standard theories tell us about sensations. Indeed, what I want, among other things, to know is what we mean by this word 'sensation'.

Let us consider first the derivative use of 'tickled', in which to say that a person is or feels tickled is to say that he is amused. What is the connexion between feeling tickled and laughing? Clearly it is not a necessary connexion, since a person who feels tickled may repress his laughter, or be so weak in lungs or throat or so busy singing that he cannot laugh.

We might try to maintain that since feeling tickled involves wanting to laugh, we want to laugh in order to banish the tickle.

Having the tickle is a cause or condition of wanting to laugh. But this certainly will not do. I do not first feel tickled and then decide that laughter would be a good remedy and then, if permitted, produce the remedial laughter. To feel tickled seems logically and not merely causally to involve having an impulse to laugh—or rather having an impulse to laugh when one must not laugh or cannot laugh or cannot laugh enough. To feel tickled either is or involves wanting to laugh, in the sense of 'want' in which a dog wants to scratch when prevented from doing so. It is not a cause of which wanting to laugh is an effect. Nor even is my laughing, if I do laugh, an effect of which my feeling tickled was the cause. For I *felt* tickled only because I could not or would not laugh. I was amused enough to laugh, but there was an obstruction to my laughing, or to my laughing enough. My feeling tickled was, more nearly, an effect of the existence of an impediment to laughing. It was amusement under duress.

To return now to the tickle that the cobweb gives me. Having or feeling the tickle, I have an impulse to scratch or rub the part of my cheek that was brushed by the cobweb. But feeling the tickle is surely not the cause of which the impulse to scratch is an effect. If I have an intolerable tickle, I have an irresistible impulse to scratch; but I am not the victim of *two* compulsions. I have elsewhere argued for the idea that a tickle just *is* a thwarted impulse to scratch, and that it is localized in my cheek, say, only in the sense that that is where I have an impulse to scratch myself. But I do not think now that this will do. The connexion between having a tickle and wanting to scratch seems to me neither a cause-effect connexion between events, nor a paraphrase-relation between expressions.

It will be noticed that, on very different levels, there is a close parallel between feeling a tickle and feeling like writing to *The Times*. Both are bound up with not-yet-satisfied inclinations to do certain things. The big difference is that the one is a primitive, unsophisticated or merely 'animal' inclination; the other is a sophisticated and acquired inclination. The former is localizable, the latter is not (save in the far-fetched sense that the indignant man's fingers may itch for the fountain-pen). It is easy to think of intermediate cases. Thirst, as the baby is thirsty, is quite unsophisticated. Thirst for a cup of hot, sweet tea demands more sophistication. The transition from feeling thirsty to feeling like drinking some hot, sweet tea and from this to feeling like going out for a country walk or feeling like writing to *The Times* seems to be a fairly smooth transition, though of course the gap between its terminals is very wide indeed. One way in which this gap develops is worth mentioning. When I feel a very unsophisticated or purely 'animal' distress, like feeling a tickle or feeling leg-weary, the things I have an impulse to do are very restricted. I have an impulse *either* to scratch *or* to rub my cheek— and that is all. Or I have an impulse *either* to dawdle *or* to sit down *or* to lie down—and that is all. But when I feel like protesting about the unfair incidence of Death Duties, either fountain-pen, or pencil or typewriter will do; and such and such phrases will do either here or there; and I might employ either this adjective or that adverb. Moreover, there are other papers than *The Times* and other ways of making protests than writing to the papers.

In a word, the behaviour of a thirsty infant or a dog with a tickle is easier to predict than that of an indignant, literate man; correspondingly, distresses of the primitive sort commonly have a local seat; while the sophisticated distresses tend not to do so. Both rank as feelings, but only the former are ordinarily called 'sensations'.

Of a battery of unsolved conceptual questions about sensations, I want here to raise one. We say that a man with a parched throat, an aching head, or an itching rash can, in certain circumstances, *forget* his discomfort. A competing excitement may totally absorb him; or by an effort of will he may concentrate his whole mind upon some other matter. The more acute his discomfort, the less likely is he to get or keep his mind on other things; his effort of will has to be the more strenuous or the countervailing excitement has to be the greater. It seems to be a tautology to say that, as his discomfort approaches torture, the difficulty of distracting his mind from it approaches impossibility.

Now if he does for a time forget his headache, should we say that his headache has stopped? Or that it has continued, but been for a time unfelt? Or that it has been felt all along, but has not for that time distressed him?

We hardly want to say that the burning house across the road was an anodyne—indeed if we did want to say this, we should not want to say that it caused the man to 'forget' his pain. In this use of 'forget', we can only forget discomforts that are still there. Nor could we well speak of the *difficulty* of distracting a person from his itches, if we did not think that in some way the itches were in competition with the jokes or anecdotes by which we try to distract him. On the other hand, we are reluctant to speak either of unfelt pains, or of felt but unnoticed pains, or of pains being both felt and noticed but (in this use) completely forgotten. So what ought we to say?

I find it harder to suggest a natural transition from 'feeling a tickle' or 'feeling like taking a nap' to the use of 'feel' followed by an adjective of general condition, like 'unfit', 'uneasy' or 'cross'. For what one is said to feel, in this use, is something so generic and, as a rule, so non-momentary that it is in sharp contrast with, for instance, tickles which are highly specific, well localized, and exist only for well-defined and short periods. But I suppose the thing might develop in this way. First, there are some kinds of bodily distresses, which are not narrowly localizable or clockable. An ache has a spread, both lateral and in depth, that a prick or a scald has not, and one may have the sensation of exhaustion or chilliness all over and all through one's body. There need be no other answer to the question 'Where do you feel slack, shivery or sore?' than 'Everywhere'. Similarly, a lot of such sensations are more or less lingering. A shooting pain is felt at a moment and for a moment, but an ache or nausea is not like that. We should not call a short, sharp pain an 'ache'.

Next, having learned to talk and understand talk about feeling particular tickles, the child can generalize this, and speak of feeling tickles all over his body or of his keeping on feeling tickles in different places. He learns to use 'feel' in ways to which the questions When? and Where? are inappropriate, since 'here, there and everywhere' and 'most of the time' are already connoted by its generalized use. When he says 'I feel uncomfortable', he knows that this covers a lot of different momentary and lingering, pin-pointed and spread discomforts. He might begin by 'my head is too hot, and the sheets are rumpled and a moment ago my nose wanted blowing', but he would soon give up the idea of presenting an inventory. It was a matter of all sorts of discomforts crowding in on one another and overlapping one another ever since he went to bed.

From this sort of generalized reference to lots of particular felt distresses, it is not a difficult transition to generalized references to distresses of the unlocalizable because sophisticated kinds. There are quite enough analogies between feeling uncomfortable in bed yesterday evening and feeling uncomfortable during a conversation about the peccadillos of one's friends, to make the use of 'feel' natural for both situations—even though in the latter situation one might be unable to specify any momentary or lingering, localizable or spread distresses that one had felt. Feeling irritated is, in lots of ways, like feeling irritations all over, even though it is unlike it in the one way, that no itches or anything like itches need be felt when one feels irritated.

What, lastly, is to be said of the expression 'to feel that something is the case'? We speak of feeling strongly that there is a flaw in the argument, but not of feeling it acutely or of feeling it distinctly or of feeling it carefully. No sort of perception or perceptual exploration is suggested, nor any sort of tolerable or intolerable distress or even freedom from distress. We can, perhaps, suggest paraphrasing the expression by 'I am (or feel) strongly inclined to say that there is a flaw in the argument' and this reminds us of the expression 'to feel like doing so and so'. But 'I feel that there is a flaw in the argument' is not quite the same thing as 'I feel like saying that there is a flaw in it'. For one thing, if I feel like taking a nap, and do take it, then, to put it crudely, the situation is restored. I do not, ordinarily, then feel like taking another nap. But if I feel that there is a flaw in the argument, and come out with the flat assertion that there *is* a flaw there, the situation is not restored. So I was not just hankering to say something; and if I do just say that there is a flaw in the argument, I still continue merely to feel that there is a flaw in it. Just saying so does not satisfy me. So perhaps we should say that to feel that something is the case is to hanker not to *say* but to believe that it is the case. But now the difficulty is that believing that something is the case is not something that we can execute or, therefore, hanker to execute. A person can be ordered to say something, but not to believe it. (This is not because believing that something is the case is an insuperably difficult task, like jumping over the moon, but because there is no such task. It is not difficult or easy to believe things.) Nor can feeling that something is the case be equated with wanting to believe that it is the case, for I can feel that the international situation has not improved though I should like to believe that it has improved. Feeling that something is the case is, in fact, not a sort of hankering at all. There is no question of it being relieved or gratified. It is more like being on a slope or having a momentum, nisus, or slide in a certain direction.

Part of the contrast between feeling that there is a flaw in your argument and thinking so seems to be this. If a person thinks so, then he can give some sort of an answer to the question why he thinks it, what sort of a flaw it is, and even perhaps whereabouts in the argument it is. But if he merely feels that it has a flaw, then of course he has no answer to such questions. He is just dissatisfied or reluctant or uneasy or suspicious. He cannot think what to say.

Most of us can never do better than feel that a joke was in bad taste, or that the shape of a Chinese bowl is exactly right. We have not got the vocabulary with which to answer questions; much less have we got the competence to make the right use of such a vocabulary. In other cases we possess the vocabulary and some of the requisite competence in using it, but have not yet mobilized it, or not adequately. At the moment I only feel that there is a flaw in your argument; but if you will hold your peace for a little while, I hope to be able to tell you, if not the flaw in the argument, at least some reason for thinking that it has one. My objections are not yet at the tip of my tongue, but they are moving in that direction. I can't yet think what to say, but it's coming.

I have said that to feel that there is something wrong is to be just dissatisfied, reluctant, uneasy, or suspicious. Now these adjectives belong to the class of adjectives of general condition. In some circumstances we should use these same adjectives in order to tell in what mood or frame of mind a person was. But here they are used in a special way for a special context; for they have what I may call 'propositional attachments'. It is one sort of thing to feel suspicious of a bridge; it is not quite the same sort of thing to feel suspicious of an argument. Reluctance to commit his weight to a bridge may characterize an elephant; reluctance to commit himself to the conclusion of an argument can characterize only an educated human being. It is, if you like, an attitude (blessed word!) not towards things in general (as depression is), nor towards a particular thing or person (as covetousness and indignation are), but towards intellectual articles such as theories, arguments, hypotheses and the like.

The transition from feeling satisfied or dissatisfied after a meal, to feeling satisfied or dissatisfied with one's treatment by the hotel servants, and from there to feeling satisfied or dissatisfied with a theory, a proof, or a piece of calculation, is, I think, though long, still a natural one, even though there is nothing corresponding to gnawing feelings in the stomach when one feels dissatisfied with, say, the Lamarckian theory of evolution.

To feel that something is the case is not the same as to feel sure that it is the case. Feeling sure is *not* feeling any qualms. Hence one can feel quite or perfectly sure; that is, feel absolutely no qualms at all. But one feels strongly (or fairly strongly or not very strongly) that something is the case; and what has some strength may always not be strong enough. I may yet find out by examination that the argument is valid after all.

There exist in English the picturesque idioms 'I feel in my bones that so and so' and 'I feel in my heart of hearts that such and such'. These idioms suggest that when we speak of feeling that something is the case, we are, sometimes, influenced by the perceptual use of 'feel', and particularly by this use in connexion with anatomically internal happenings and conditions. The analogy works, apparently, in two or three distinct ways. (*a*) What I detect when I feel my heart palpitating is something which you cannot detect in any way, and not easily or conveniently in any other way. My report is that of a solitary uncorroborated reporter. (*b*) But it is also a virtually incontrovertible report. My way of detecting the palpitations does not involve steps or apparatus or clues or indications. The palpitations are not diagnosed or inferred but felt—and that is good enough, because it is as good as anything could be. (*c*) But detection by feeling also has something unsatisfactory about it; namely, that feeling is constitutionally imprecise—imprecise as judged by the standards officially set by sight. If, in the dark, I have to tell the time by feeling the hands of the clock with my fingers, I cannot determine the exact time, as I can when I can see the clock. And my position is much worse if I can feel the hands of the clock only with my elbow or my toes. Anatomically internal things, though detected, sometimes, with the highest reliability, are also detected with gross nebulousness. We cannot say in our ordinarily fairly precise terms what we detect by feeling, because what we detect in that way is itself incurably blurred. It is like trying to catch a jelly-fish on a fish hook. Now when we report that we feel that so and so is the case, our reports are, in a somewhat similar way, also solitary, uncorroborated, incontrovertible, and too blurred to be made articulate. When I feel that there is something amiss with an argument, I do not yet *see* what is wrong with it. If I did see what was wrong with it, then, of course, I could say what was wrong with it, and if I could say this, then 'feel' would no longer be the verb to use. 'Feel' goes with 'can't quite say'. Note that it is not a case of something being too delicate to be caught by our gross linguistic tools, but of its being too amorphous to be caught by our over-delicate linguistic tools. (Sometimes we say that an argument *smells* bad or that a promise *rings* untruly. Smelling and hearing are also inferior ways of perceiving. They warn us vaguely of things which we would prefer to have a good look at if only we could.)

One further point. For a person to feel that there is something wrong with an argument, he must have heard or read the argument and understood or misunderstood it. An infant could not feel that there was a flaw in an argument or that the orator was being insincere. We need training to be capable of feeling that something is the case. But feeling that something is the case is not something that we execute or perform or accomplish. It is not a piece of trying (like considering), or an achievement (like finding or solving). Now some theorists who enjoy multiplying faculties, speak of Sense, Reason, and Intuition as different faculties, and part of what they have in mind when they speak of Intuition is such facts as that husbands sometimes feel that their wives are worried, connoisseurs feel that the shape of a Chinese bowl is just right, and generals feel that the moment for the counter-attack has arrived.

The inarticulateness of such feelings is, of course, just what is wanted to set apart the elevated and inscrutable findings of Intuition from the mundane and scrutinizable findings of Reason. Now this sort of talk is obviously silly. But it is true that some people's 'noses' can be relied on in some sorts of matters; namely, when they are intelligent people, with a good deal of practice in matters of this sort. The directions in which they are inclined to move, though they cannot say why, tend to turn out to have been the right directions. If a schoolgirl feels that 'Eclipse' will win the Derby, we should not be influenced; if a shepherd, of ripe years, feels that there will be a storm, we should take our raincoats with us; if a wife feels that her husband is out of sorts, he probably is, unless she is very newly married or very silly; and if the dealer feels that the picture is genuine, while the collector feels that it is a fake, we had better look up their records before taking sides.

Feeling, in this use, is not a magical way of getting the answers to questions, alternative to calculating, cross-examining, weighing pros and cons, and so on. It is not a way of getting answers at all. It is not something that can be done cautiously or recklessly, skilfully or clumsily, for it is not something that is done. None the less, the hunches of a person who is experienced and judicious in the right matters are generally, not always, the right hunches to ride. And if he and we did not ride hunches, we should never move at all; though equally, if we merely rode hunches without doing any careful work as well, we should seldom get to a destination and never get our hunches educated. In every move we make, theoretical or practical (or æsthetic, etc.), we are putting some trust in our 'noses'. What matters is whether our 'noses' have become or been made trustworthy.

It is not even always requisite or desirable that a person should try to move on from feeling that something is the case to producing an articulate case for it being so. It is the business of the judge, but it is not the business of the members of the jury to give reasons for a verdict. Their business is to give the right verdict, not to satisfy a Court of Appeal that it was the right verdict to give. Nor, necessarily, should the general prepare himself to satisfy critics that he chose the right moment for the counter-attack. He might be a good general but a bad lecturer at the Staff College; there is no contradiction in saying that he had good reasons for ordering the counter-attack at that moment, though he could not then or subsequently tell himself or anyone else what they were. We are all pretty much in his position in the business of sizing up people's characters. Our goodness or badness at making such estimates need not and does not vary concomitantly with our goodness or badness at producing justifications for them.

It is a philosophical misfortune that, partly under the influence of tripartitionism, many theorists have assimilated feeling-that to emotion, as though the possession of strategic flair or a cultivated taste in ceramics were akin to being a chronic worrier or being easily vexed or scared. The hapless artist seems to have suffered the worst from this muddle. He is sometimes alleged to be having some emotion or other (other than that of being thoroughly interested in his job) whenever he is doing his work; or at least to be in some unexplained way reviving or recalling some emotion that he has previously had. And if he is any good, then the effect of his work on those who listen to his music, read his stories, or look at his pictures or dining-room chairs, is that they too are induced to have this emotion. Which particular emotions these are, is usually left unspecified; presumably because we should only have to mention such emotions as boredom, jealousy, restlessness, irritation, and hilarity in order to make the whole story sound as ridiculous as it is. (Nameless æsthetic emotions are sometimes called in at this point to save the theory's face.)

We do properly use the phrase 'feel that' in reporting exercises of taste, and we do properly use the verb 'feel' in reporting such things as agitations and tranquillities. But to say that a person feels that something is the case is not to give any answer at all to the questions 'How does he feel?' and 'In what mood is he?' though answers to these questions are often required to explain why judgments in matters of taste or elsewhere are perverted.

CHAPTER V

THE EXPRESSION THEORY OF ART

By O. K. Bouwsma

THE expression theory of art is, I suppose, the most commonly held of all theories of art. Yet no statement of it seems to satisfy many of those who expound it. And some of us find all statements of it baffling. I propose in what follows to examine it carefully. In order to do this, I want first of all to state the question which gives rise to the theory and then to follow the lead of that question in providing an answer. I am eager to do this without using the language of the expression theory. I intend then to examine the language of that theory in order to discover whether it may reasonably be interpreted to mean what is stated in my answer. In this way I expect to indicate an important ambiguity in the use of the word 'expression', but more emphatically to expose confusions in the use of the word 'emotion'. This then may explain the bafflement.

I

And now I should like to describe the sort of situation out of which by devious turnings the phrase 'expression of emotion' may be conceived to arise.

Imagine then two friends who attend a concert together. They go together untroubled. On the way they talk about two girls, about communism and pie on earth, and about a silly joke they once laughed at and now confess to each other that they never understood. They were indeed untroubled, and so they entered the hall. The music begins, the piece ends, the applause intervenes, and the music begins again. Then comes the intermission and time for small talk. Octave, a naïve fellow, who loves music, spoke first. 'It was lovely, wasn't it? Very sad music, though.' Verbo, for that was the other's name, replied: 'Yes, it was very sad'. But the moment he said this he became uncomfortable.

73

He fidgeted in his seat, looked askance at his friend, but said no
more aloud. He blinked, he knitted his brows, and he muttered
to himself. 'Sad music, indeed! Sad? Sad music?' Then he
looked gloomy and shook his head. Just before the conductor
returned, he was muttering to himself, 'Sad music, crybaby,
weeping willows, tear urns, sad grandma, sad, your grandmother!' He was quite upset and horribly confused. Fortunately,
about this time the conductor returned and the music began.
Verbo was upset but he was a good listener, and he was soon
reconciled. Several times he perked up with 'There it is again',
but music calms, and he listened to the end. The two friends
walked home together but their conversation was slow now and
troubled. Verbo found no delight in two girls, in pie on earth,
or in old jokes. There was a sliver in his happiness. At the corner
as he parted with Octave, he looked into the sky, 'Twinkling
stars, my eye! Sad music, my ear!' and he smiled uncomfortably.
He was miserable. And Octave went home, worried about his
friend.

So Verbo went home and went to bed. To sleep? No, he
couldn't sleep. After four turns on his pillow, he got up, put a
record on the phonograph, and hoped. It didn't help. The
sentence 'Sad, isn't it?' like an imp, sat smiling in the loud-speaker.
He shut off the phonograph and paced the floor. He fell asleep,
finally, scribbling away at his table, like any other philosopher.

This then is how I should like to consider the use of the phrase
'expression of emotion'. It may be thought of as arising out of
such situations as that I have just described. The use of emotional
terms—sad, gay, joyous, calm, restless, hopeful, playful, etc.—in
describing music, poems, pictures, etc., is indeed common. So
long as such descriptions are accepted and understood in inno-
cence, there will be, of course, no puzzle. But nearly everyone
can understand the motives of Verbo's question 'How can music
be sad?' and of his impulsive 'It can't, of course'.

Let us now consider two ways in which one may safely escape
the expression theory.

Imagine Verbo at his desk, writing. This is what he now writes
and this gives him temporary relief. 'Every time I hear that music
I hear that it's sad. Yet I persist in denying it. I say that it cannot

be sad. And now what if I were wrong? If every day I met a
frog, and the frog said to me that he was a prince, and that there
were crown jewels in his head ("wears yet a precious jewel in his
head"), no doubt I should begin by calling him a liar. But the
more I'd consider this the more troubled I should be. If I could
only believe him, and then treat him like a prince, I'd feel so
much better. But perhaps *this* would be more like the case of
this music: Suppose I met the frog and every day he said to me, "I
can talk," and then went on talking and asked me, "Can I talk?"
then what would I do? And that's very much how it is with the
music. I hear the music, and there it is again, sad, weeping. It's
silly to deny this. See now, how it is? There's a little prince, the
soul of a prince, in the frog, and so there's the soul in this music,
a princess, perhaps. See then how rude I was denying this
princess her weeping. Why shouldn't music have a soul too?
Why this prejudice in favour of lungs and livers? And it occurs
to me that this is precisely how people have talked about music
and poems. Art lives, doesn't it? And how did Milton describe a
good book? Didn't Shelley pour out his soul? And isn't there
soul and spirit in the music? I remember now that the poet
Yeats recommended some such thing. There are spirits; the air
is full of them. They haunt music, cry in it. They dance
in poems, and laugh. Pan-psychism for the habitation of all
delicacies! So this is how it is, and there is neither joke nor
puzzle in this sad music. There's a sad soul in it.'

And then it was that Verbo fell asleep. His resistance to the
music had melted away as soon as he gave up his curious prejudice
in favour of animal bodies, as soon as he saw that chords and tones,
like rhymes and rhythms, may sigh and shed invisible tears.
Tears without tear glands—oh, I know the vulgar habit! But
surely tones may weep. Consider now how reasonable all this
is. Verbo is suddenly surprised to discover something which
he has always known; namely, that music is sad. And the discovery
startles him. Why? Because in connexion with this, he thinks
of his sister Sandra (Cassie to all who saw her cry). And he
knows what her being sad is like. She sobs, she wipes her eyes,
and she tells her troubles. Cassie has a soul, of course. So Cassie
is sad and the music is sad. So the question for Verbo is 'How
can the music be like Cassie?' and he gives the answer 'Why

F

shouldn't there be a soul of the music, that flits in and flits out (People die too!) and inhabits a sonata for a half-hour? Or why shouldn't there be a whole troupe of them? "The music is sad" is just like "Cassie is sad", after all. And Octave who was not disturbed was quite right for he must have a kind of untroubled belief in spirits. He believes in the frog-prince, in the nymphs in the wood, and in the psyche of the sonnet.'

This then is one way of going to sleep. But there is another one, and it is based upon much the same sort of method. Both accept as the standard meaning for 'The music is sad', the meaning of 'Cassie is sad'. We saw how Verbo came to see that the meaning is the same, and how then it was true in the case of the music. He might however have decided that the meaning certainly was the same, but that as applied to the music it simply made no sense at all, or was plainly false. Souls in sonnets! Don't be silly. There is the story about Parmenides, well known to all readers of Dionoges,[1] which will illustrate the sort of thing I have in mind. According to the story, Parmenides and his finicky friend Zeno once went to a chariot race. The horses and chariots had been whizzing past and the race had been quite exciting. During the third round, at one turn a chariot broke an axle and horse and chariot and rider went through the fence. It was a marvellous exhibition of motion done to a turn at a turn. Parmenides was enjoying himself thoroughly. He clutched at the railing and shouted at the top of his voice, 'Go, Buceph! Run!' The race is close. But at about the seventh round, with Buceph now some part of a parasang behind, Parmenides began to consider: 'Half the distance in half the time; a quarter of the length of a horse in a quarter of the pace it takes. . . '. Suddenly, before the race was half over, Parmenides turned to Zeno. 'Zeno', he said, 'this is impossible.' Zeno, who was ready for his master, retorted, 'I quit looking a long time ago'. So they left the chariot race, a little embarrassed at their non-existence showing as they walked, but they did not once look back to see how Buceph was doing.

This then is the story about Parmenides. It may be, of course, that this story is not true; it may be one of Dionoges' little jokes. But our concern is not with Parmenides. The point is that it illustrates a certain way of disposing of puzzles. Parmenides has

---

[1] An author of no repute at all, not to be confused with Diogenes.

been disciplined to a certain use of such words as 'run', 'go', 'turn', 'walk', etc., so that when he is thoughtful and has all his careful wits about him, he never uses those words. He is then fully aware that all forms of motion are impossible. Nevertheless, the eyes are cunning tempters. In any case, as soon as Parmenides reflects, he buries himself in his tight-fitting vocabulary, and shuts out chariots and horses, and Buceph, as well. 'Motion is impossible, so what am I doing here? Less than nothing. N'est pas is not.' This disposition of the puzzle is, of course, open only to very strong men. Not many of those people who believe in the impossibility of motion are capable of leaving a horse race, especially when some fleet favourite is only a few heads behind.

Now something like this was a possibility also for Verbo. When, puzzled as he was, asking 'How can that be?' he hit upon the happy solution 'Why not?' But he might surely have said, stamping his foot, 'It can't be'. And in order then to avoid the pain of what can't be, he might have sworn off music altogether. No more concerts, no more records! The more radical decision is in such cases most effective. One can imagine Parmenides, for instance, sitting out the race, with his eyes closed, and every minute blinking and squinting, hoping he'd see nothing. So too Verbo might have continued to listen to music, but before every hearing invigorating his resolution never to say that the music was sad. Success in this latter enterprise is not likely to be successful, and for anyone who has already been puzzled it is almost certainly futile.

We have now noticed two ways in which one may attempt to rid oneself of the puzzle concerning 'The music is sad', but incidentally we have also noticed the puzzle. The puzzle is identified with the question 'How can music be sad?' We have also noticed how easy it is, once having asked the question, to follow it with 'Well, it can't'. I want now to go on to consider the expression theory in the light of the question 'How can it be?' In effect, the expression theory is intended to relieve people who are puzzled by music, etc. They listen and they say that the music is sad. They ask, troubled and shaking their heads, 'How can it be?' Then along comes the expression theory. It calms them, saying, 'Don't you see that the music expresses sadness and that this is

what you mean by it's being sad?' The puzzled one may be
calmed too, if he isn't careful. In any case, I propose to consider
the question 'How can it be?' before going on further.

This question, 'How can it be?' is apparently then not a
question primarily about the music. One listens to the music and
hears all that there is to hear. And he is sure that it is sad. Nevertheless, when he notices this and then returns to the music to
identify just what is sad in it, he is baffled. If someone, for
instance, had said that there is a certain succession of four notes
on the flute, in this music, and he now sought to identify them,
he could play the music, and when they came along, he would
exclaim, 'There they are', and that would be just what he aimed
at. Or again if someone had said that a certain passage was very
painful, and he explained that he meant by this that when it is
heard one feels a stinging at one's finger tips, then again one
could play the music and wait for the stinging. Neither is it
like the question which leaped out of the surprise of the farmer
at the birth of his first two-headed calf. He looked, amazed, and
exclaimed, 'Well, I'll be switched! How can that be?' He bedded
the old cow, Janus, tucked in the calf, and went to consult his
book. He did not stand muttering, looking at the calf, as Verbo
did listening to the record on the phonograph. He took out his
great book, *The Cow*, and read the chapter entitled 'Two Heads
Are Better than One?' He read statistics and something about
the incidence of prenatal collusion and decided to keep an eye on
collaborators among his herd. And that was all. When now it
comes to 'The music is sad', there's no such easy relief. What is
there to listen for? What statistics are there?

We have noticed before how Verbo settled his difficulty. He
did this, but not by examining the music any further. He simply
knew that the music was sad, and supplied the invisible tears, the
unheard sobs, the soul of the music. If you had asked him to
identify the tears, the unheard sobs, the soul of the music, he
could not have done this. He might have tried, of course, and
then he would have been baffled too. But the point is that he
tries to think of the sadness of the music in the way in which
he thinks of Cassie's sadness. Now we may be ready to explain
the predicament, the bafflement. It arises from our trying to
understand our use of the sentence 'The music is sad' in terms

of our uses of other sentences very much like this. So Verbo understands in terms of the sentence 'Cassie is sad'. One can imagine him saying to himself, 'I know what sadness is, of course, having Cassie in the house, so that must be how it is with the music'. Happily, as in the case of Parmenides, he thought of only one use, and as with a sharp knife he cut the facts to suit the knife. But suppose now that there are several uses of sentences much like 'The music is sad'; what then? Is it like this use or this use or this use? And suppose that sometimes it's like this and at other times like this, and sometimes like both. Suppose further that one is only vaguely aware that this is so, and that one's question 'How can that be?' is not stated in such a way as to make this possibility explicit, would it then be any wonder that there is bafflement?

Let us admit then that the use of 'The music is sad' is baffling, and that without some exploration, the question 'How can that be?' cannot be dealt with. Merely listening to the music will not suffice. We must then explore the uses of other sentences which are or may be similar to this, and we may hope that in this process we may see the expression theory emerge. At any rate, we'll understand what we are about.

2

What now are some of these other types of sentences which might be helpful? Well, here are a few that might serve: 'Cassie is sad', 'Cassie's dog is sad', 'Cassie's book is sad', 'Cassie's face is sad'. Perhaps, one or the other of these will do.

Though we have already noticed how Verbo came to use 'Cassie is sad', I should like to consider that sentence further. Verbo understood this. When, as he remembered so well, the telephone call came and little Cassie answered—she had been waiting for that call—she was hurt. Her voice had broken as she talked, and he knew that the news had been bad. But he did not think she would take it so hard. And when she turned to him and he asked her what the man had said, at first her chin quivered and she didn't speak. Then she moved towards him and fell into his arms, sobbing: 'Poor Felicia, poor Felicia!' He stroked her hair and finally, when she was calm, she began to

pour out her confidences to him. She loved her cat so; they
had been brought up together, had had their milk from the same
bottle, and had kept no secrets from each other. And now the
veterinary had called to say that she had had another fit. And
she burst into tears again. This·was some years ago. Cassie is
older now.

But this is not the only way in which 'Cassie is sad' is used.
Verbo had often heard his father and mother remark that it was
good that Cassie could cry. They used to quote some grandmother who made a proverb in the family. It went: 'Wet pillows
are best'. She had made this up many years ago when some
cousin came to sudden grief. This cousin was just on the verge
of planned happiness, when the terrible news came. (Her picture
is the third in the album.) She received the news in silence and
never spoke of it or referred to it as long as she washed the
dishes in her father's house, for, as you may have guessed, she
never married. She never cried either. No one ever heard her
sniffling in the middle of the night. She expressed no regrets.
And she never told cat or mirror anything. Once she asked for
a handkerchief, but she said she had a cold. All the family knew
what had happened, of course, and everyone was concerned, but
there was nothing to do. And so she was in many ways changed.
She was drooping, she had no future, and she tried to forget her
past. She was not interested. They all referred to her as their
sad cousin, and they hoped that she would melt. But she didn't.
Yet how can Cassie's cousin be sad if she never cries?

Well, there is a third use of 'Cassie is sad'. Tonight Cassie,
who is eighteen now, quite a young lady, as the neighbours say,
goes up to her room with her cat, her big book, and a great bowl
of popcorn. She settles into her chair, tells kitty to get down,
munches buttery corn, and reads her book. Before very long she
is quite absorbed in what she reads and feels pretty bad. Her
eyes fill with tears and the words on the page swim in the pool.
It's so warm and so sweet and so sad! She would like to read this
aloud, it's so wonderful, but she knows how the sadness in her
throat would break her words in two. She's so sorry; she's so
sad. She raises her eyes, closes them, and revels in a deep-drawn
sigh. She takes up a full hand of popcorn and returns to her
sadness. She reads on and eats no more corn. If she should sob

in corn, she might choke. She does sob once, and quite loud, so that she is startled by it. She doesn't want to be heard sobbing over her book. Five minutes later she lays her book aside, and in a playful mood, twits her cat, pretending she's a little bird. Then, walking like old Mother Hubbard, she goes to the cupboard to get her poor cat a milk.

Cassie is sad, isn't she? Is she? Now that you consider it, she isn't really sad, is she? That cosy chair, that deliberate popcorn, that playing sparrow with her cat, that old Mother Hubbard walk—these are not the manners of a sad girl. She hasn't lost her appetite. Still one can see at once how we come to describe her in this way. Those are not phony tears, and she's as helpless in her sobs and in keeping her voice steady and clear as she was years ago when her dear cat had that fit. And she can, if you are so curious, show you in the book just what made her feel so sad. So you see it is very much like the case in which Cassie was sad. There's an obvious difference, and a similarity too. And now if you balk at this and don't want to say that Cassie in this situation is sad, your objection is intelligible. On the other hand, if Cassie herself laughingly protests, 'Oh, yes, I was sad', that will be intelligible too. This then may serve as an illustration of the way in which a puzzle which might become quite serious is fairly easily dealt with. How can Cassie be sad, eating popcorn and playing she's a sparrow?

In order to make this clear, consider Cassie now a grown woman, and an accomplished actress. She now reads that same passage which years ago left her limp as a willow, but her voice is steady and clear, and there are no tears. She understands what she reads and everyone says that she reads it with such feeling—it's so sad!—but there isn't a sign of emotion except for the reading itself, which, as I said, goes along smoothly and controlled even to each breath and syllable. So there are no wet eyes, no drunken voice, and not a sob that isn't in the script. So there. Is she sad? I take it not. The spoken words are not enough. Tears, real tears, a voice that breaks against a word, sighs that happen to one, suffered sobs—when the reading occasions these, then you might say that Cassie was sad. Shall we say, however, that the reading is sad? How can that be? Well, you see, don't you?

Let us now attend to a sentence of a different type: 'Cassie's dog is sad'. Can a dog be sad? Can a dog hope? Can a dog be disappointed? We know, of course, how a Cartesian would answer. He might very well reply with this question, 'Can a locomotive be sad?' Generous, he might allow that a locomotive might look sad, and so give you the benefit of a sad look for your dog. But can a dog be sad? Well, our dog can. Once during the summer when Cassie left her for three weeks, you should have seen her. She wouldn't look at the meatiest bone. She'd hang her head and look up at you as woebegone as a cow. And she'd walk as though her four hearts would break. She didn't cry, of course, and there were no confidences except those touching ones that come by way of petting and snuggling and looking into those wailing eyes. In any case, our dog acted very much like that sad cousin who couldn't cry. She had plenty of reason, much too much, but she kept her wellings-up down. It's clear, in any case, what I mean when I say that our dog was sad. You mustn't expect everything from a sad dog.

So we pass to another type of sentence: 'Cassie's book is sad'. Well, obviously books don't cry. Books do not remember happier days nor look upon hopes snuffed out. Still, books that are sad must have something to do with sadness, so there must be sadness. We know, of course. Books make people sad. Cassie reads her book and in a few minutes, if she's doing well, she's sad. Not really sad, of course, but there are real tears, and one big sob that almost shook the house. It certainly would be misleading to say that it was imaginary sadness, for the sadness of Cassie isn't imagined by anyone, not even by herself. What she reads, on the other hand, is imaginary. What she reads about never happened. In this respect it's quite different from the case in which she is overwhelmed by the sad news over the telephone. That was not imaginary, and with the tears and sobs there was worry, there was distress. She didn't go twittering about, pretending she was a little bird five minutes after that happened. So a sad book is a book that makes Cassie, for instance, sad. You ask, 'Well, what are you crying about?' And she says, 'Booh, you just read this'. It's true that that is how you will find out, but you may certainly anticipate too that it will be a story about a little boy who died, a brave little boy who had stood up bravely for his father, about a new love and reconciliation come almost too late, about a parting of friends and tender feelings that will die, and so on. At any rate, if this is what it is like, you won't be surprised. It's a sad book.

There is one further sentence to consider: 'Cassie's face is sad'. The same sort of thing might be said about her speaking, about her walk, about her eyes, etc. There is once again an obvious way of dealing with this. What makes you say her face is sad? Anyone can tell. See those tear stains and those swollen eyes. And those curved lines, they all turn down. Her face is like all those sad faces in simple drawings where with six strokes of my neighbour's pencil I give you 'Sad-Eye, the Sorry Man'. The sad face is easily marked by these few unmistakable signs. Pull a sad face, or droop one, and then study it. What have you done? In any case, I am supposing that there is another use of 'Cassie's face is sad', where this simplicity is absent. Oh, yes, there may be certain lines, but if you now ask, 'And is this all you mean by Cassie's face being sad?' the answer may very well be 'No'. Where then is the sadness? Take a long look and tell me. Cassie, hold still. The sadness is written all over her face, and I can't tell you it's here and not there. The more I look, the more I see it. The sadness in this case is not identified with some gross and simple signs. And you are not likely to find it there in some quick glance. Gaze into that face, leisurely, quietly, gently. It's as though it were composed not of what is sad in all sad faces, but rather of what is sad only in each sad face you've ever known. This sad face is sad but when you try now to tell someone what is sad in it, as you might with the drawing I made, you will have nothing to say. But you may say, 'Look, and you will see'. It is clear, of course, that when Cassie's face is sad, she need not be sad at all. And certainly when you look as you do, you need not be sad.

We have noticed briefly several types of sentences similar to 'The music is sad', and we have seen how in respect to several of these the same sort of puzzling might arise that arose in respect to 'The music is sad'. We have also seen how in respect to these more obvious cases this puzzling is relieved. The puzzling is relieved by discerning the similarity between the offending use and some other use or uses. And now I should like to ask whether the puzzle concerning 'The music is sad' might not also be relieved in some similar fashion. Is there not a use of some type of sentence, familiar and relatively untroubled, which is like the use of 'The music is sad'?

We have these types of sentences now ready at our disposal: There are two uses of 'Cassie is sad', in the first of which she is concerned about her cat, and in the second of which she is cosy and tearful, reading her book. We have 'Cassie's cousin is sad', in which Cassie's cousin has real cause but no tears, and 'Cassie's dog is sad', in which her dog is tearless as her cousin, but with a difference of course. You could scarcely say that Fido restrained his tears. Then there were the uses of 'Cassie's face is sad' and 'Cassie's reading is sad'. And, of course, there is the use of 'Cassie's book is sad'. I am going to take for granted that these uses are also intelligible. Now then is the use of 'The music is sad' similar to any of these?

I suppose that if the question is stated in this way, one might go on by pointing out a similarity between it and each one of these other types of sentences. But what we must discover is enough similarity, enough to relieve the puzzle. So the question is: To which use is the use of 'The music is sad' most similar? Certainly not to 'Cassie is sad (about her cat)', nor to 'Cassie's cousin is sad', nor to 'Cassie's dog is sad'.

There are two analogies that one may hopefully seize upon. The first is this: 'Cassie is sad, reading a book,' is very much like 'Verbo is sad, listening to music'. And this first is also very much like 'Cassie is sad, hearing the news over the telephone'. And just as the first involves 'The book is sad', so the second involves 'The music is sad', and the third involves 'The news is sad'. Now let us consider the first. Reading the book is one thing, and feeling sad is quite another, and when you say that the book is sad, you mean by this something like this: When Cassie reads, she feels sad about what she reads. Her feeling sad refers to her tears, her sobs, etc. So too listening to the music and hearing it is one thing, and feeling sad is another, and when you say that the music is sad, you mean that while Verbo listens to the music, he feels sad. And shall we add that he feels sad about it? This might, if you like, refer to something like his half-tears, sub-sobs, etc.

Suppose now we try to relieve Verbo in this way. We say, 'Don't you see? "This music is sad" is like "The book is sad". You understand that. That's very much like "The news is sad".' Will that satisfy him? I think that if he is very sharp, it won't. He may say, 'I can see how "The book is sad" is like "The news is sad". But when it comes to these you can easily point out the disturbance, the weeping, but the music—that's different. Still there might be something.' What now bothers him?

I think what bothers him may be explained in this way. When you say that a book is sad, or a certain passage in a book is sad, you may mean one or other or both of two things. You may mean what has already been defined by the analogy above. But you may also mean something else. The following illustration may exhibit this. Imagine Cassie, then, in her big chair, reading, and this is the passage she reads:

'I say this in case we become bad', Alyosha went on, 'but there's no reason why we should become bad, is there, boys? Let us be, first and above all, kind, then honest, and let us never forget each other! I say that again. I give you my word, for my part, that I'll never forget one of you. Every face looking at me now I shall remember even for thirty years. Just now Kolya said to Kartashov that he did not care to know whether he exists or not. But I cannot forget that Kartashov exists and that he is blushing now as he did when he discovered the founders of Troy, but is looking at me with his jolly, kind, dear little eyes. Boys, my dear boys, let us all be generous and brave like Ilusha, clever, brave and generous like Kolya (though he will be ever so much cleverer when he grows up), and let us all be as modest, as clever and sweet as Kartashov. But why am I talking about those two! You are all dear to me, boys, from this day forth I have a place in my heart for you all, and I beg you to keep a place in your hearts for me! Well, and who has united us in this kind, good feeling which we shall remember, and intend to remember all our lives? Who, if not Ilusha, the good boy, the dear boy, precious to us for ever! Let us never forget him. May his memory live for ever in our hearts from this time forth.'

Cassie reads this and Cassie cries. Let us call this Cassie's sadness. But is there now any other emotion, any other sadness, present? Well, there may very well be. There may be the Alyosha emotion. Whether that is present, however, depends upon how the passage in question is read. It may be read in such a way, that though Cassie understands all she reads, and so knows about the Alyosha emotion, yet she will miss it. This will be the case if she cries through the reading of it. If she reads the passage well, controlled, clear, unfalteringly, with feeling, as we say, which does not mean with crying, then the Alyosha emotion will be present. Otherwise only signs of it will be present. Anyone who has tried to read such a passage well, and who has sometimes failed and sometimes succeeded, will understand what I have in mind. Now then we have distinguished the Cassie emotion and the Alyosha emotion. They may be present together, but only, I think, when the Cassie emotion is relatively weak. And so when someone says that the passage in question is sad, then in order to understand we must ask, 'Is it sad in the Cassie emotion or is it sad in the Alyosha emotion?'

And now we are prepared again to examine the analogy: 'The music is sad' is like 'The book is sad', where it is sad with the Alyosha emotion. This now eliminates the messiness of tears. What we mean by Alyosha's emotion involves no tears, just as the sadness of the music involves no tears. And this now may remind us of Cassie reading the passage, cool, collected, reading with feeling. But more to the point it suggests the sentence 'Cassie's face is sad'. For see, when the music is sad, there are no tears, and when the passage is read, well read, there are no tears. And so when I look into this face and find it sad, there are no tears. The sadness in all these cases may be unmistakable, and yet in none of these is there anything to which I might now draw your attention, and say, 'That's how I recognize it as sad'. Even in the case of the reading, it isn't the sentences, it isn't the subject, that make it sad. The sadness is in the reading. Like a musical score, it too may be played without feeling. And it isn't now as though you both read and have these feelings. There is nothing but the reading, and the feeling is nothing apart from this. Read the passage with and without feeling, and see that the difference consists in a difference in the reading. What baffles in these cases is that when you use the word 'sadness' and the phrase 'with feeling', you are certain to anticipate sadness and feeling in the ordinary sense. But if the sadness is in the sounds you make, reading or playing, and in the face, once you are fore-warned you need no longer anticipate anything else. There is sadness which is heard and sadness which is seen.

This then is my result. 'The music is sad' is like 'The book is sad', where 'The book is sad' is like 'The face is sad'. But 'The music is sad' is sometimes also like 'The book is sad', where 'The book is sad' is like 'The news is sad'. If exhibiting these analogies is to be helpful, then, of course, this depends on the intelligibility of such sentences as 'The book is sad', 'The face is sad', 'The news is sad', etc.

3

So far I have tried to do two things. I have tried to state the problem to which the expression theory is addressed, and then I have gone on to work at the solution of that problem in the way in which this statement of the problem itself suggests that it be worked out. In doing this I have sought deliberately to avoid the language of the expression theory.

Here then is the phrase to be studied. The expression theory maintains: The music is sad means: The music is the expression of sadness or of a certain sadness. The crucial word is the word 'expression'. There are now at least two contexts which determine the use of that word, one is the language of emotion, and the other is the language of or about language.

Let us consider first the use of the word 'expression' in the language of emotion. In the discussion of the types of sentences above, it will be remembered that Cassie's cousin is sad, but doesn't cry. She does not 'express' her emotion. Cassie, on the other hand, carries on, crying, sobbing, and confiding in everyone. She 'expresses' her emotion, and the expression of her emotion is tears, noises, talk. That talk is all about her cat, remember. When she reads her book, she carries on in much the same way. In this latter case, there was some question as to whether there was really any emotion. She was so sad, remember, and ate popcorn. But in terms of what we just now said, whether there is emotion or not, there certainly is 'expression' of emotion. These tears are just as wet as other tears, and her sobs are just as wet too. So in both cases there is expression of emotion, and in the first case there is emotion, thick as you please, but in the second case, it's not that thick. It appears, then, that you might find it quite natural to say that there is expression of emotion but no emotion, much as you might say that there was the thought of an elephant, but no elephant. This may not seem

so strange, however, if we reflect that as in the case of Cassie's
cousin, there may be emotion, but no or very little expression of
emotion.

In order to probe the further roots of the uses of this phrase,
it may be useful to notice that the language of emotion is
dominantly the language of water. So many of our associations
with the word 'emotion' are liquid. See then: Emotions well
up. Children and young girls bubble over. There are springs of
emotion. A sad person is a deep well. Emotions come in waves;
they are like the tides; they ebb and flow. There are floods and
'seas of passion'. Some people gush; some are turbulent. Anger
boils. A man blows up like a boiler. Sorrow overwhelms.
The dear girl froze. We all know the theory of humours. In
any case, it is easy enough, in this way, to think of a human
being as like a reservoir and an everflowing pool and stream of
emotions. All flow on toward a dam, which may be raised or
lowered, and over and through which there is a constant trickle.
Behind the dam are many currents, hot, cold, lukewarm, swift,
slow, steady, rippling, smooth. And there are many colours.
Perhaps we should say that currents are never exhausted and do
not altogether trickle away. Emotions, like our thoughts, are
funded, ready to be tapped, to be rippled, to be disturbed.

Let us see how the term 'expression' fits into this figure. How
was it with Cassie's cousin? Well, once there was a clear, smooth-
flowing current of affection, and it flowed, trickle, trickle, over
the dam in happy anticipation and a chestful of hope's kitchen
and linen showers. And suddenly a planet falls, in the form of a
letter, into that deep and flowing pool. Commotion follows,
waves leap, eddies swirl. The current rushes on to the dam.
And what happens? The dam rises. Cassie's cousin resists, bites
her lip, intensifies her fist. She keeps the current back. Her grief
is impounded. She does not 'express' her emotion. And what
happened to Cassie, when she felt so bad about the cat? That's
easy. Then too there was a disturbance. The current came down,
splashed over the dam which did not rise at all, and it flowed
away in a hurly-burly of 'Oh! It's awful! My poor kitty!'
Cassie let herself go. She 'expressed' her emotion.

The use of the word 'expression' in the light of this figure is,
I take it, clear enough. And the use of the word in this way

describes a familiar difference in the way in which good news and bad news may affect us. And now we may ask, 'And is it something like this that people have in mind when they say that art is the expression of emotion?' Certainly something like this, at least part of the time. Consider how Wordsworth wrote about poetry: 'Poetry is the spontaneous overflow of powerful emotions'. Overflow! This suggests the pool and the dam and the 'powerful' current. An emotion, lying quiet, suddenly gets going and goes over. There is spontaneity, of course. No planet falls and no cat is sick. The emotion is unprovoked. There is also the common view that artists are people who are more emotional than other people. They are temperamental. This once again suggests the idea that they have particular need of some overflow. Poetry is a little like blowing off steam. Write poetry or explode!

This isn't all that Wordsworth said about poetry. In the same context he said: 'Poetry is emotion recollected in tranquillity'. Again this suggests a hiding place of emotion, a place where past heartaches are stored, and may be taken up again, 'recollected'. We store ideas. We also put away emotions. So we have the pool as we had the pool before in describing Cassie's cousin and Cassie. But now we have something else, 'the spontaneous overflow' and the 'recollection in tranquillity'.

Let us consider this for a moment, again in order to notice the use of the word 'expression'. Cassie hears bad news and cries. She 'expresses' her emotion. The emotion is aroused and out it flows. What now happens in the case of the poet? Ostensibly in his case too emotions are aroused, but they do not flow out. Poets do not cry enough. Emotions are stored up, blocked. Emotions accumulate. And what happens now? Well, one of two things may happen. Emotions may quite suddenly leap up like spray, and find a way out, or again a poet may dip into the pool with his word dipper, and then dip them out. It's as though the emotions come over the dam in little boats (the poems) and the little boats may be used over and over again to carry over new surges. And this too may be described in this way: The poet 'expresses' his emotion. Cassie cries. The real incident is sufficient. The poet does not cry. The real incident is not sufficient. He's got to make poems in order to cry. All men must cry.

This may seem a bit fantastic, but this sort of phantasy is common in explaining something as old, for instance, as Aristotle's use of the word 'catharsis'.

The analogy which we have tried to exhibit now is this one: As Cassie 'expresses' her emotion at hearing the news, so the poet or reader 'expresses' his emotion at reading the poem. The news and the poem arouse or evoke the respective emotions. Now most people who expound the expression theory are not content with this analogy. They say that Cassie merely vents or discharges her emotion. This is not 'expression' of emotion. Cassie merely gets rid of her emotion. And what does the poem do? Perhaps in terms of our figure we may say: It ripples it, blows a gentle wind over it, like a bird skimming the water. At any rate the emotion stays. And so the theory seeks a more suitable analogy and finds it conveniently in the language about language.

I should like first to notice certain distinctions which lead to this shift from the first to the second analogy. In the first place poems and music are quite different from the occasions that make Cassie and Cassie's cousin so sad. Tones on a piano and a faithless lover or a dying cat are not much alike, and this is enough to disturb the analogy. But there is also an unmistakable difference in the use of the word 'emotion' in the two cases. An 'emotion recollected in tranquillity' is, after all, as I suggested before, more like a ripple than like a tempest. It is, accordingly, these distinctions that determine the shift. It may be useful to notice that the general form of the first analogy is retained in the second. For the poem and the music are still conceived as 'arousing', as 'evoking', the emotion.

The new analogy accordingly is this one: Music 'expresses' sadness (art expresses emotion) as sentences 'express' ideas. And now, I think, it is easy to see why this analogy should have been seized upon. In the first place so much of art involves symbols, sentences themselves, and representations. There are horses in pictures. It is quite easy then to fall into regarding art as symbolic; that is, as like sentences. And now just as sentences symbolize ideas and serve to evoke them as distinguished from real things, of which ideas are more like shadows, so too music and poems serve to evoke emotions of a peculiar sort, emotions which are like the shadows of real emotions. So this analogy is certainly an improvement. Art is after all an artifice, like sentences, and the emotions involved are related to the real things in much the way that ideas are to real things, faint copies. All this fits in very well with the idea that art is like a dream, a substitute of real life, a vicarious more of what you cannot have, a shadowland.

And now how does this analogy succeed?

Before answering this question, I should like to notice the use of the words 'evoking' and 'arousing'. Sentences 'evoke' ideas. As one spieler I know says: 'When I read a sentence, an idea pops into my head'. Pops! This is something like what, according to the analogy, is meant by sentences 'expressing' ideas. I am not interested in criticizing this at this point. I wish only to clarify ideas. Pop! Consider the sentence 'The elephant ate a jumbo peanut'. If at the moment when you read this sentence you see in your mind's eye a big elephant nuzzling around a huge peanut, this will illustrate what 'evoking' is like. The sentence evokes; the idea pops. There is the sentence and there is this unmistakable seeing in your mind's eye. And if this happened, surely you would have got the idea. What I wish to point out is that it is this view or some similar view of how sentences work, that underlies this present analogy. They 'evoke'. But the word 'evoke' has other contexts. It suggests spirits, witchcraft. The spirit of Samuel appearing at the behest of the witch of Endor is an 'evocation'. Spiritualistic mediums 'evoke' the living spirits of the dead. And the point of this association is that the spirits are waiting, in the second or third canto of Dante's *Comedy*, perhaps, to be called. They are in storage like our ideas, like our emotions. And the word 'arouse' is like the word 'evoke'. Whom do you arouse? The sleeper. And so, sleeping ideas and sleeping emotions lie bedded in that spacious dormitory—hush!— we call the mind. Waiting to be called! And why now have I made a point of this? Because this helps to fill out this analogy by which in particular we are led to use the word 'feeling' or 'emotion' in the language of the expression theory. The music 'evokes', 'arouses' feelings.

Now then, do poems and music and pictures evoke emotions as sentences evoke images? I think that they frequently do. Cassie reading her book may be cited as an instance. This seems to me a very common type of experience. It happens at the movies, in

G

reading novels, and even in listening to music. People are moved to tears. If, accordingly, the expression theory were intended merely to describe experience of this sort, I should say, 'Very well'. In that case there would be no particular puzzle, beyond presenting this analogy clearly. But I, at least, am convinced that this is not all.

The difficulty, then, does not arise concerning experiences of this sort. The puzzle arises and remains most stubbornly where the sadness is dry-eyed. And here the analogy with language seems, at least, to be of no use. Cassie may read the passage with feeling, but without the flicker of an eyelash. And she may listen to sad music as cool and intent as she is gazing at a butterfly. She might say that it was more like watching, fascinated, the pain in a suffering face, herself quite undistressed. Santayana identifies the experience in this way: 'Not until I confound the impressions (the music, the sentences) and suffuse the symbols with the emotions they arouse, and find joy and sweetness in the very words I hear, will the expressiveness constitute a beauty. . . .'.[1] I propose now to study this sentence.

Now notice how curious this is. Once more we have the sentences or the music. And these arouse emotion. This describes Cassie reading her book. So we might expect that Cassie would cry and would sob and so on. But this isn't all. Cassie is confused. Actually she is crying but she thinks the words are crying. She wipes her tears off those words. She sighs but the words heave. The sentence of Santayana suggests that she sees the sentences she reads through her tears and now her tears misserve her much as blue moods or dark glasses do. So Cassie looks through sadness and the sentence is tearful. What a pathetic fallacy! From confusion to suffusion! Are there misplaced emotions? Imagine what this would be like where sentences aroused not emotions but a toothache. And now you confused the toothache with the sentence, and before someone prevented you, you sent the sentence to the dentist.

Nevertheless, Santayana has almost certainly identified an experience that is different from that in which Cassie is sad over her book. We find 'joy and sweetness in the very words' we hear. Clearly, too, Santayana has been misled by these words

[1] *Sense of Beauty* (1896), p. 149.

'joy and sweetness'. For if there is joy and sweetness, where should these be but where they usually are? Where is joy then and where is sweetness? In the human breast, in the heart ('my heart leaps up when I behold'), in the eye. And if you say this, then indeed there must be some illusion. The sentence is like a mirror that catches and holds what is in the heart. And so artful are poets' sentences that the best readers are the best confused. I want now, however, to suggest that indeed joy and sweetness, and sadness too, are in the very words you hear. But in that case, joy and sweetness must be of the sort that can be in sentences. We must, accordingly, try to figure out what this 'joy and sweetness in the very words' is like. For even though, making a mistake, one imagined they were in the words, their being there must make some sense. And Santayana too does not imagine that sentences cry.

Let me return now to the analogy: The music is sad is like: The sentence expresses an idea. We saw before how the sentence 'The elephant ate a jumbo peanut' might be accompanied by an image and how this was like sentences or music arousing emotions. We want now to see how we might use the phrase 'joy and sweetness in the very words'. Do we have a meaning for 'The idea in the very words you hear'. Where is the idea of the elephant eating a jumbo peanut? Suppose we say, 'It's in the very words you hear'. Have you ever seen, in your mind's eye, that is, an elephant eating a peanut in the very words you hear? A sentence is like a circus tent? I do not suppose that anyone who said that joy and sweetness are in the very words you hear would be likely to say that this was like the way in which you might also see an image in the very sentence which you hear— a bald head in the word 'but'. I should like in any case to try something different.

I do not intend to abandon the analogy with language yet. Music is expression of emotion as sentences are expression of ideas. But now how do sentences express ideas? We have noticed one way in which sentences do sometimes have meaning. Sentences, however, have been described in many ways. Sentences are like buzzers, like doorbells, like electric switches. Sentences are like mirrors, like maps, like pictures; sentences are like road signs, with arrows pointing the way. And so we might go on to ask, 'Is music like buzzers, like pictures, like road sign arrows?' I do not however intend to do this. It will be noticed that the same analogy by which we have been trying to understand music, art, etc., may serve us also to understand what language is like. The analogy presupposes that we do know something about music, and so turning the analogy to this use may be fruitful. It might show us just how enlightening and how unenlightening the analogy is.

In order to study the analogy between music and the sentence and to try in this way to find out what the sentence is like, I now intend to offer a foolish theory. This may throw into clearer relief what Santayana says. What is understanding a sentence like? Understanding a sentence is speaking the sentence in a certain way. You can tell, listening to yourself talk, that you are understanding the sentence, and so can anyone else who hears you speak. Understanding has its rhythm. So the meaning of the sentence consists in a certain reading of the sentence. If, in this case, a sentence is spoken and not understood by someone, there would be only one thing to do; namely, speak the sentence again. Obviously this account will not do for there are other ways of clarifying what we mean. Nevertheless, in some cases it may be all that is necessary.

Now notice. If this were what the meaning of a sentence is like, we should see at once what was meant if someone said that the meaning or the idea is in the sentence. For if there is meaning, where could it be but in the sentence, since the sentence is all there is? Of course, it is true that the sentence would have to be spoken and, of course, spoken in some way or other. And with every variation in reading it might then be said to have a different meaning. If anyone asked, 'And what does the sentence mean?' expecting you to point to something or to elaborate the matter in gestures or to translate, it would be clear that he quite misunderstood what meaning is like. One might even correct him, saying it is even misleading to say that the meaning is in the sentence, as though it were only a part of the sentence, or tucked away somehow under overlapping syllables. A sentence having meaning in a case like this would be something like a living thing. Here too one might ask, 'Where is the life in a squirrel and in a geranium?' Truly the life is the squirrel and is the geranium and is no part of either nor tucked away in some hidden fold or tiny vein. And so it is with the sentence, according to our imaginary theory. We might speak of the sentence as like a living thing.

And now let us see whether we have some corresponding use for 'The joy and sweetness are in the very words you hear'. People do ask about the meaning of poems and even about the meaning of music. Let us first of all say that the meaning is 'the joy and sweetness', and the sadness. And where are these? In the very words you hear, and in the music. And now notice that what was admittedly a foolish theory in respect to sentences is not a foolish theory in respect to poems or music. Do you get the poem? Do you get the music? If you do not, pointing, gestures, translations will not help. (Understanding the words is pre-supposed.) There will be only one thing to do; namely, read the verses again, play the music once more. And what will the joy and sweetness and the sadness be like? They will be like the life in the living thing, not to be distinguished as some one part of the poem or music and not another part, or as some shadow that follows the sounded words or tones. 'In the very words you hear,' like the squirrel in fur!

I infer now that the analogy between the 'joy and sweetness' in words and the meaning in sentences is misleading and is not likely to be helpful. The meaning of sentences is translatable, but the 'meaning' of poems, of music, is not. We have seen how this is so. There may, of course, be something in the sounding of all sentences which is analogous to the 'joy and sweetness in the very words', but it is nòt the meaning of those sentences. And now this is an interesting consequence. It makes sense to ask, 'What does the sentence express?' It expresses a meaning, of course, and you may have some way of showing what this is, without using the sentence to do so. But now it makes no sense to ask, 'What does the poem express?' or 'What does the music express?' We may say, if we like, that both are expressive, but we must beware of the analogy with language. And we may prevent the helpless searching in this case, by insisting that they 'express' nothing, nothing at all.

And now let us review. My assumption has been that the expression theory is plagued with certain analogies that are not clearly distinguished, and none of which finally is helpful without being misleading. The first analogy is that in terms of which we commonly think of emotions. The second is that in terms of which we think of language, the doorbell view. Besides this there are two different types of experience that arise in connexion with art. One of these types may be fairly well described by the analogy with doorbell language. The similarity of our language, however, in respect to both these types of experience, conceals the difference between those two types. Santayana's sentence reveals the agony that follows the recognition of this difference in these types of experience and the attempt to employ the language which describes the one to describe the other. The language requires very interesting translation. My conclusion, accordingly, is this: The analogy drawn from language may be useful in describing one type of experience. It is practically useless in describing the other. Since, then, these two analogies dominate the use of the word 'expression', I suggest that, for the sake of clarity and charity, they be abandoned in seeking to describe that 'expressiveness' which Santayana says constitutes 'a beauty'.

If we now abandon these analogies, are we also to abandon the use of the word 'expression'? Not unless we please to do so. But we do so at our risk, for these analogies are not easily abandoned. We may, however, fortify our use of this word by considerations such as these. We use the word 'expressive' to describe faces. And we use 'expressive' in much the same way that we use the phrase 'has character'. A face that is expressive 'has character'. But when we now say that a face has character, this may remind us that the letters of the alphabet are characters. Let us suppose for a moment that this is related to 'He's a character!' I suppose that he's a character and he has a character do not mean quite the same thing. There are antics in he's a character. Try again: The zig-zag line has character and the wavy line has character. Each letter of the alphabet is a character, but also has character. The number tokens, 1 2 3 4 5 6 7 8 9—each has its character. In the same way sounds have character. Let me see whether we can explain this further. You might say that if some dancing master were to arrange a dance for each of the numbers, you might see how a dance for the number one would not do at all

for number five. Or again if the numbers were to be dressed in
scarfs, again a certain colour and a certain flimsy material would
do for six but would not suit five at all. Now something of the
same sort is true of words, and particularly of some. Words have
character. I am tempted to say that all these things have their
peculiar feel, but this then must be understood on the analogy
with touch. If we, for instance, said that all these things have
their peculiar feeling, then once again it might be supposed that
in connexion with them there is a feeling which is aroused by
them.

Let your ears and your eyes, perhaps, too, feel these familiar
bits of nonsense:

> Hi diddle diddle!
> Fee! fi, fo, fum!
> Intery, mintery.
> Abra ca da bra.

Each has its character. Each is, in this sense, expressive. But to
ask now 'What is its character or what does it express?' is to fall
into the pit. You may, of course, experiment to exhibit more
clearly just what the character, in each case, is. You may, for
instance, contrast the leaping, the stomping, the mincing, the
shuffle, with what you get if you change the vowels. Try:

> Ho! doodle doodle!
> Fa, fo, fu, fim!
> Untery, muntery.
> Ay bray cay day bray.

One might also go on to change consonants in order again to
exhibit character by giving the words new edges and making their
sides steeper or smoothing them down.

I do not intend, in proposing illustrations of this sort, to suggest
that art is nonsense and that its character is simple as these syllables
are. A face, no doubt may bear the impress, the character, of a
life's torment and of its hope and victory. So too words and
phrases may come blazing out of the burning past. In art the
world is born afresh, but the travail of the artist may have had
its beginnings in children's play. My only point is that once the
poem is born it has its character as surely as a cry in the night
or intery, mintery. And this character is not something that

follows it around like a clatter in a man's insides when he reads
it. The light of the sun is in the sun, where you see it. So with
the character of the poem. Hear the words and do not imagine
that in hearing them you gulp a jigger to make yourself foam.
Rather suppose that the poem is as hard as marble, ingrained, it
may be, with indelible sorrow.

If, accordingly, we now use the sentence 'Art is expression',
or 'Art is expressive', and the use of this sentence is determined
by elucidations such as I have just now set out, then, I think that
our language may save us from some torture. And this means
that we are now prepared to use freely those sentences that the
expression theory is commonly inclined to correct. For now,
unabashed, we shall say that the music is sad, and we shall not go
on to say that this means that the music expresses sadness. For
the sadness is to the music rather like the redness to the apple,
than it is like the burp to the cider. And above all we shall not,
having heard the music or read the poem, ask, 'What does it
express?'

4

And now it's many words ago since we left Verbo and his
friend at the corner. Verbo was trying to figure out, you remember, how the music was related to his grandmother. How can
music be sad? I suggested then that he was having word trouble,
and that it would be necessary to probe his sentences. And so we
probed. And now what shall we tell Verbo?

Verbo, we will say, the music is sad. And then we will remind
him that the geranium is living, and that the sun is light. We will
say these things so that he will not look away from the music
to discover the sadness of it. Are you looking for the life in the
geranium? Are you looking for the light in the sun? As then
the life and the light describe the geranium and the sun, so too
does sadness describe the music. And then we shall have to go on
to tell him about these fearful analogies, and about Santayana's
wrestle on the precipice. And about how we cut the ropes! And
you may be sure that just as things are going along so well,
Verbo will ask, flicking the ashes from his cigarette, 'And what
about the sadness?'

And now it's time to take the cat out of the bag, for so far all that has been exposed is the bag. The sadness is a quality of what we have already described as the character, the expressive. One piece of music is like and unlike some other pieces of music. These similarities and these differences may be perceived. Now then, we have a class of sad music. But why sad; that is, why use this word? It must be remembered, of course, that the use of this word is not precise. So there may be some pieces of music which are unmistakably sad, and others which shade off in gradations to the point where the question 'Is it sad?' is not even asked. Suppose we ask our question 'Why sad?' in respect to the unmistakable cases. Then, perhaps, some such answer as this will do. Sad music has some of the characteristics of people who are sad. It will be slow, not tripping: it will be low, not tinkling. People who are sad move more slowly, and when they speak, they speak softly and low. Associations of this sort may, of course, be multiplied indefinitely. And this now is the kitten in whose interest we made so much fuss about the bag. The kitten has, I think, turned out to be a scrawny little creature, not worth much. But the bag was worth it.

The bag was worth it? What I have in mind is that the identification of music as the expressive, as character, is crucial. That the expressive is sad serves now only to tag the music. It is introspective or, in relation to the music, an aside. It's a judgment that intervenes. Music need not be sad, nor joyous, nor anything else. Æstheticians usually account for this by inventing all sorts of emotions without names, an emotion for every piece of music. Besides, bad music, characterless music, the unexpressive, may be sad in quite the same way that good music may be. This is no objection, of course, to such classifications. I am interested only in clarifying the distinction between our uses of these several sentences.

And now that I have come to see what a thicket of tangle-words I've tried to find my way through, it seems to me that I am echoing such words as years ago I read in Croce, but certainly did not then understand. Perhaps if I read Croce again now I shouldn't understand them either. 'Beauty is expression.'

CHAPTER VI

A STUDY OF THE IRREFUTABILITY OF TWO ÆSTHETIC THEORIES

By Beryl Lake

THE aim of this paper is to study the linguistic nature of two famous æsthetic theories, those of Benedetto Croce and Clive Bell. I am interested in beginning to understand (at least) what sort of functions statements in æsthetics have. Do they, for example, like the statement 'Living grass is green', describe matter of fact which could be different, and could, therefore, serve to refute them? Or do they, like 'A panther is an animal', assert a classification in *a priori* terms, that is do we find that 'Art is significant form' is both irrefutable and unconfirmable by reference to any facts about works of art?

The usual assumption seems to be that a theory of æsthetics describes the nature of art and artistic experience, in a way not very different from that in which a scientific theory describes the nature of physical phenomena; that a theory of æsthetics is based upon, and answers to, matter of fact, albeit very special and sacred matters of fact about Art. This is the assumption I am particularly interested in examining.

CROCE'S THEORY ABOUT WORKS OF ART

I shall begin by asking what sort of theory this is, and then I shall go on to consider what sort of theory Bell's is. This will involve expounding the theories in so far as they describe the nature of works of art, as briefly as possible, and considering whether they are empirically refutable.

Croce distinguishes between two kinds of knowledge, intuitive or imaginative, and intellectual or conceptual. Works of art are primarily examples of what he calls 'intuitive knowledge', so this is the kind of knowledge which will concern us here. Intuitive knowledge is direct knowledge of individuals, including images. It is also active (not passive reception of sensations); the knower somehow creates what he knows. Intuitions (occasions of intuitive knowledge) are furthermore identified with expressions:

> The spirit only intuits in making, forming, expressing. . . .[1]

Intuitions must also be something like perceptions: Croce gives the examples of 'this river, this lake, this brook . . .' as intuitions, to be contrasted with the *concept* water.[2] Croce's emphasis on the similarity between intuitions and perceptions is not so puzzling if one remembers that on his view any perception is an activity; both what we would call perception and imaginative activity are creative.

Now, real works of art are not physical objects at all, in spite of our everyday way of speaking about them, *i.e.* despite such comments as 'I saw a Van Gogh hanging on the wall', and 'The Philharmonic Orchestra plays Brahms' second symphony'. Croce insists that real works of art do not hang on the walls of galleries nor are they performed by orchestras, but exist in the minds of all who truly appreciate them. They consist in imaginatively organized non-physical wholes; they are syntheses and clarifications of crude sensory material, that is of the impressions of sense. Sense experience, it is suggested, is given form in intuition:

> The impressions reappear as it were in expression, like water put into a filter, which reappears the same and yet different on the other side.[3]

Briefly, then, the part of Croce's *Æsthetic* with which we are concerned is that which asserts:

1. The real work of art is an imaginative, or spiritual, or mental, not a physical thing.
2. The real work of art is an intuition which is also an expression and an occasion of intuitive knowledge. This 'knowledge' is not knowledge about anything; it is immediate.

Many difficulties arise, which are frequently pointed out. For one thing, it is hard to see what 'expression' means if it is not expression at least in some sort of physical medium. But we shall not enter into a detailed account of possible flaws in Croce's

---

[1] Benedetto Croce, *Æsthetic* (London 1922), p. 8.
[2] *Ibid.*, p. 22.   [3] *Ibid.*, p. 15.

theory; rather, we shall attempt to understand what sort of theory it is, *i.e.* whether or not it is empirical.

Let us suppose that it is empirical. The claim is that a work of art is an imaginative entity, an intuition-expression, existing only in the minds of artists and genuine appreciators. Picasso's 'Guernica' is not really in the New York Museum of Modern Art; only its incidental physical medium is. Picasso's 'Guernica' is what Picasso intuited and what bona fide viewers appreciate. It is unlikely that all such viewers should have the same intuitions as Picasso; for since Croce holds that intuiting is creative, each person will express his own particular synthesis of his own particular impressions in his intuition. If this theory is empirical, then, one thing it claims is that certain physical objects which are usually mistaken for works of art are not works of art at all, but that somehow connected with these physical impostors are the real works of art, the sets of imaginative experiences in the life histories of all sorts of different people. No painted canvas, for example, is a real work of art. Botticelli's 'Birth of Venus', as a work of art, is some-one's intuition. Originally it was Botticelli's intuition, and the suggestion is that he had created a work of art quite apart from creating it *in a physical medium* by painting. It is incidental to the work of art proper that it should be made an object for public perception, as it were, by a manipulation of materials.

How are we to decide that it is either true or false to say that real works of art are spiritual entities of some sort and not physical objects? Suppose we find evidence from the writings of critics and artists which indicate that the mere physical-object result of the artist's intuition is not really the work of art. We might interpret, for example, Shelley's statement in his *Defense of Poetry* as a point in favour of Croce's view:

the most glorious poetry that has ever been communicated to the world is probably a feeble shadow of the original conceptions of the poet. . . .[1]

We might also cite Mozart's descriptions of pre-creative images of his works, descriptions which give the impression that his works of art were created before he set to work in a physical medium. And doubtless there are many other better examples of this kind of thing. Perhaps we could then go on to say that

---

[1] Percy Bysshe Shelley, *The Defense of Poetry* (London 1906), p. 193.

ordinary language (*e.g.* statements like 'I have just bought a beautiful Greek vase') misleads, that the common opinion that frescoes are painted walls, and that symphonies are physical sound patterns, is a false one.

But it seems that appeal to the facts relevant to this interpretation go against Croce's view at least as much as they confirm it. For example, critics speak of colour tones and formal designs in paintings, and seem to take careful note of physical elements like brush strokes. Artists make comments which imply the importance of the nature of the physical medium in which they work. Picasso said:

> I don't know in advance what I am going to put on the canvas, any more than I decide in advance what colours to use.[1]

In the case of literature, words, which are the physical medium, seem to be the vehicle of the artist's inspiration; it does not seem to be the case, as the Crocean view would imply, that a poem is an intuition which is separable from its verbal embodiment. To quote from Collingwood:

> The artistic activity does not use a ready-made language, it 'creates' language as it goes along.[2]

A poem uses language in such a way that the use is uniquely fitting for the purpose, and one might be allowed to say that the poem *is* language used creatively. The consequence of interpreting Croce's view about the nature of works of art as empirical then, seems clearly to be that it is false, since his view does not account for the fact that artists, critics and ordinary language unequivocally imply that works of art are *at least* physical objects (in the wide sense of 'physical object' usually associated with 'physical', where 'physical' covers processes as well as objects).

It looks, then, that if we interpret Croce's view as empirical we can point to facts that seem to falsify it as well as to facts that tend to confirm it. And this is not the same as saying that works of art are sometimes physical objects and sometimes not, as, for example, we might say (trivially) that works of art are sometimes paintings and sometimes not. It seems to amount to saying that, depending upon how you look at the matter, works of art are

---

[1] Quoted by Herbert Read, *Art Now* (New York 1934), p. 123.
[2] R. G. Collingwood, *The Principles of Art*, p. 275.

physical objects or they are not. Someone who considers such a
fact as that a monkey looking at a Cézanne can *with point* be said
not to be seeing a work of art, but only a physical object, may be
led to the conclusion that works of art are not physical objects,
simply because he is impressed with the differences. On the
other hand, someone else who is impressed by the fact that what
we appraise and what artists create is at least a physical object,
not a mental image (we do not normally count intuitions or
beautiful day-dreams as works of art, at least until they are
transformed into paintings, music, statues, etc.) may be led to the
opposite conclusion that works of art are physical, even if they
do differ in important respects from ordinary pens and houses
and sounds.

The question is, whether Croce intends merely to point out a
set of facts about works of art which suggests that they are
different from physical objects, and whether he would admit that
another set of facts might show that they are nevertheless
physical.

What he writes in his book *Æsthetic* suggests strongly that the
answer is no. Let us consider his theory again. 'Art' always means
primarily 'intuitive knowledge'. 'Intuitive knowledge' is so
described that it is 'knowledge by acquaintance' except that it is
always imaginative; hence a work of art *must* be imaginative
rather than material. On his theory there is no question whatever of admitting that in any sense a work of art could be a
physical object, since he insists that a work of art is an intuition,
an active creation of the imagination. Even if he did accept the
statement that a work of art is a physical object, his admission
would have to be reinterpreted in conformity with the rest of his
idealist position; for, as we noted above, all perception is in
Croce's philosophy essentially creative. Of course, if seeing a
chair is to be interpreted as a kind of imagining of a chair, as a
psychological contributing to what is seen, this goes as much
against the common belief that chairs are there to be seen as
Croce's theory goes against the common belief that works of art
are there to be seen, or heard, or understood.

It begins to look, then, as if Croce intends his theory to be
construed in a way which leaves us at a loss to know what might,
even in theory, count against it. If we say: 'But very often indeed

people believe that a work of art is *at least* painted canvas, or sculptured marble, or a pattern of sounds, which it makes sense to say many people see or hear in the same way,' Croce can answer either that it makes sense to say that a work of art is only what is appreciated and expressed in the imaginations of artists and sensitive appraisers; or that seeing painted canvas or hearing sounds is essentially creative, *i.e.* that the viewer or hearer creates what he sees or hears. In fact, both ways of speaking, Croce's and the opposite, seem to be important and acceptable. Yet if these theories are empirical, one would be false, the other true. But what could be a *conceivable* refutation of Croce? Suppose we urged that if a work of art were not a physical object in the common-sense meaning of 'physical', not, for example, paint on canvas which 'is there' for everyone to see, then there would seem to be no point whatsoever in people flocking to art galleries and concert halls, no point in summer pilgrimages to Florence or attendance at Art Festivals. For surely all that is located in Florence or concert halls that could be relevant is a collection of physical statues, buildings, paintings, or a collection of musicians, instruments, scores producing sounds, also physical. If works of art are intuitions which anyone with sufficient imagination can create, why do people not sit in the seclusion of the humblest homes to enjoy them? This, as a criticism of Croce's theory, seems simply absurd; one can imagine a number of ways in which he could answer it. He might say that of course what we are calling material works of art are the occasions for intuitions, or the guides to recreating in the imagination the artists' intuitions. It is at this point that it seems clear that Croce's view is irrefutable. We can refuse to agree, we can give reasons for our refusal along the lines indicated above, but we cannot prove him wrong, as we could prove someone wrong who wished to hold that all works of art were paintings. In the latter case we could appeal to common language and opinion: the dictionary could be our arbiter. Croce does not seem merely to be denying what is commonly said by way of criticism, since what is commonly said can be used to back his theory as well as an opposing one.

Let us suppose someone says: 'All works of art are paintings'. He will be immediately corrected: 'Oh no, some are statues, some are buildings, some are musical compositions, and so on. Look in your dictionary'. If he resists, either he will be considered obstinate in the face of refutation, or else we shall think he means something like: 'I think only paintings deserve the name of works of art'. In the latter case no rational argument is possible. We might, perhaps, try to persuade him that he does not *really* think any such thing; but it is to be presumed he knows what he thinks. Suppose, now, someone says: 'All works of art are really objects of the imagination'. We might say, 'Oh no, they are really physical objects'. Reasons can be produced on both sides, but it seems that at no point could we say that we have shown to Croce's satisfaction that his view is false. The way people talk about works of art provides evidence for both sides, but neither side will accept the opposing evidence. The Crocean could always say, 'Of course, works of art are often talked about as if they were physical objects, but this is the fault of language and does not show my view to be mistaken'.

Neither, it may be observed, will any amount of scrutinizing works of art provide us with a possible way of refuting Croce's view. Attempting to conduct the experiment of looking long and hard at a Whistler with the idea of seeing whether it is really a material or an imaginative object would not yield any result. Both Croce and a critic who holds the common belief that it is paint on canvas (albeit expertly put on and very pleasing, etc.) would have the same object to scrutinize. No facts known to the one would be unknown to the other, and there is nothing which one could point out which would convince the other that the view of which he was convinced was wrong.

We can imagine no situation in which Croce would appear irrational if he refused to give up his theory. There is no imaginable change in the world which he would grant would falsify 'Works of art are objects of the imagination'. Suppose there was a world in which there was nothing which answered to any descriptions now given of human imagination. Would Croce in this case admit that the only remaining account of works of art would be that they are physical objects? Indeed not, since without imagination, on his view, there could not be any works of art at all. The claim, 'Works of art are objects of the imagination,' stands in sharp contrast to a genuine empirical assertion, like 'Works of art are paintings'. The latter, though in fact false, could conceivably be true, *e.g.* in a world where there was no other artistic activity besides painting.

It seems that we are justified in concluding that Croce's account of the nature of works of art is not empirical, or that it is in an important way irrefutable; and it does not seem to describe a matter of fact characteristic of such works, as we tried to suggest it might when we were supposing it empirical. It does not seem to do this because counter-evidence would not turn the view into a merely probable one, nor would it refute it by showing that the view held only for a limited class of works of art.

It now looks as if Croce's theory is couched in *a priori* terms, stated in such a way that no counter-evidence can possibly be brought against it which would make him modify or reject his conclusion. It looks as if Croce is insisting that the word 'Art' *should* be restricted to the kind of intuitions he describes, although normally it is not. 'Art is Intuitive Knowledge' becomes, on this interpretation, *a priori* true, irrefutably true.

I shall go on to discuss Clive Bell's theory before considering what more (besides creating necessary propositions) these æstheticians are doing; obviously there is something more, or else æsthetics would not be the intriguing subject that it is.

CLIVE BELL'S THEORY ABOUT WORKS OF ART

Clive Bell is his own best brief expositor:

The starting point for all systems of æsthetics must be the personal experience of a peculiar emotion. The objects which provoke this emotion we call works of art.[1]

This emotion is called the æsthetic emotion; and if we can discover some quality peculiar to all the objects that provoke it, we shall have solved what I take to be the central problem of æsthetics. We shall have discovered the essential quality in a work of art. . . .[2]

This essential quality of works of art, Bell decides, is 'significant form'. Certain relations between forms, forms themselves, lines and colours are what stir our æsthetic emotions. If we ask which relations, etc., do this, the answer is, the significant ones.

---

[1] Clive Bell, *Art* (London 1927), p. 6.   [2] *Ibid.*, p. 7.

And if we ask, 'Significant of what?' the answer is given by Bell's 'metaphysical hypothesis', that they are significant ultimately of the reality of things, of 'that which gives to all things their individual significance, the thing in itself, the ultimate reality'.[1]

The claim is first made that there exist æsthetic emotions which are only aroused by works of art. Then it is claimed that what is common to all works of art, or objects which arouse æsthetic emotions, is 'significant form'.

The assertion that sensitive people have æsthetic emotions is surely empirical. We should confirm or falsify this by asking those who are acknowledged to be sensitive people whether they experience an emotion which is unique to situations in which they are appraising works of art. We are not concerned here with the truth of this claim, but simply with its semantic type, *i.e.* its empirical or *a priori* character. And it certainly seems to be empirical. Many people would be prepared to admit that there is an æsthetic emotion, although some may wish to say that natural objects as well as works of art arouse it. We can believe that if Clive Bell had been confronted with constant denials of the existence of the æsthetic emotion he could still sincerely claim that he frequently experienced it. His experience at least would back his claim that such experiences do exist, and as a matter of fact many others admit having emotions of this sort. Yet we believe that Bell would say that if he had never had such an experience, his æsthetic theory would not have arisen; he insists that this personal emotion is the starting point. Bell's theory, then, seems to have what we might call empirical feet on the ground. But from there it soars into what we might call metaphysical heights, and the same suspicion assails us as in the case of Croce's view.

What is common to all the works of art, or objects which arouse the æsthetic emotion, is significant form. Bell never explains clearly what significant form is; the 'metaphysical hypothesis' suggests that it is not merely a certain (unspecified) combination of lines and colours. (Bell concerns himself, as is evident, primarily with painting.) Roger Fry, who shared Bell's view, commented that significant form is more than pleasing

[1] *Ibid.*, pp. 69–70.

patterns and so on, but that an attempt at full explanation would land him 'in the depths of mysticism': 'On the edge of that gulf I stop'.[1] As Wittgenstein's famous comment advises, 'Whereof one cannot speak, thereof one must be silent'.[2]

Whatever significant form is, the questions here are 'What are we to make of the view that it is the common denominator of works of art?' 'In what position would a person be if he denied it?'

This is a way of asking if the view is empirical. How could someone convince Clive Bell that works of art (supposing, for the sake of argument, they have a common feature) do not have significant form as an essential feature, or never have significant form at all. Someone might say that Frith's 'Paddington Station' is a work of art which, because it is purely descriptive of reality, has no significant form, and therefore Bell's view is false. But we know what Bell's answer would be; he gives it himself. 'Paddington Station' is *not* a work of art precisely because it does not have significant form, precisely because it is merely descriptive painting.[3] His critical judgments and his æsthetic theory seem to be in line. Apropos of the frequent praise he bestows on Cézanne in his critical works, he writes:

> Cézanne carried me off my feet before I ever noticed that his strongest characteristic was an insistence on the supremacy of significant form. When I noticed this, my admiration for Cézanne and some of his followers confirmed me in my æsthetic theories.[4]

Bell is impressed with the formal qualities of paintings. He says:

> The pure mathematician rapt in his studies knows a state of mind which I take to be similar, if not identical . . . [with the æsthetic emotion aroused by significant form].[5]

Any painting, then, which someone might try to point out as an example of art which does not have significant form, would be denied to be a work of art for this very reason. No instance could possibly be produced of a work of art which did not have significant form, for anything which did not have significant form would not be counted as a work of art. 'Paddington

[1] Roger Fry, *Vision and Design* (London 1920), p. 302.
[2] Ludwig Wittgenstein, *Tractatus Logico-Philosophicus* (London 1947), p. 189.
[3] Bell, *op. cit.*, pp. 17–18.   [4] *Ibid.*, pp. 40–1.   [5] *Ibid.*, p. 25.

Station' has not significant form; therefore, in spite of popular belief to the contrary, 'Paddington Station' is not a work of art. Likewise, since 'Paddington Station', Bell judges, is not worthy of the title 'work of art', it cannot have significant form. The upshot of the theory is that nothing can count as a work of art unless it has significant form. It begins to look as if 'Works of art have significant form' is like 'Squares have four sides'. 'Is a work of art' and 'has significant form' seem to mean the same, so that the latter does not say what anything must answer to in order to count as a work of art, except that it must be a work of art.

Certainly someone who wishes to deny that all works of art have significant form would not be able to produce any evidence to convince Bell. He might point to a Hogarth and say that it lacked significant form but was a work of art, but Bell would reply that either it has significant form or it is not a work of art. He might point to a Ben Nicholson and say that it had significant form but was not a work of art, or, for that matter, to a tree. But Bell is committed to the view that if something has significant form it is a work of art, and if something is a work of art, it has significant form. No exceptions are theoretically possible once his view is adopted. This is not the characteristic of an empirical view.

We can imagine water running uphill, but we cannot begin to imagine, according to Bell, a work of art which has no significant form. Adopting his view clearly amounts to deciding not to call anything which we do not also call 'significant form', 'work of art'. We are reminded of the way in which we refuse to call anything 'square' which we do not also call 'four-sided'. It looks as if 'only those paintings, etc., are works of art which have significant form' is irrefutable, therefore non-empirical, and therefore in some sense *a priori*.

Of course, such sentences as 'Works of art have significant form' do not in ordinary language express *a priori* propositions. But then the expression 'significant form' is not an ordinary expression. There is reason for supposing that æstheticians have, in one sense, a special language adapted to the purposes of their own theories. Bell, for example, coined this phrase to establish his point that there is something which is very important to him about works of art. But he goes on to make it impossible to give an instance of even a purely imaginary thing which is both a work of art and lacks significant form.

CONCLUSIONS

I have tried to show that Croce's and Bell's theories are not refutable by reference to matters of fact. It seems to me that Croce will allow nothing to count as an example of a work of art which is not what he calls an intuition, and Clive Bell will allow nothing to count as an example of a work of art which has not what he calls significant form. While it certainly sounds as if both these writers are describing an objective characteristic which all works of art have, study of their theories reveals that this is not true, since no imaginable instance will count against their descriptions.

Let us suppose that Croce and Clive Bell disagree together about whether a work of art is an intuition or something which has significant form. One point of disagreement would be that while Croce would emphasize that a painting is a product of the æsthete's imagination, Clive Bell would emphasize that its formal characteristics, the relation of its lines and shapes as they are painted on the canvas, are Significant. Suppose Croce tried to convince Bell that the paint on the canvas was incidental, that what was appreciated was something in the imagination of the appreciator; he might point out that this is the difference between a physical object and a work of art. Bell would undoubtedly retort that the difference between a physical object and a work of art is that a work of art is a physical object which has a certain sort of form, significant form. We can easily see that the argument would be interminable, neither being able to convince the other. This does not happen in empirical disputes. For example, a dispute about whether or not the word 'art' is, as a matter of fact, used only for paintings would be terminated by consulting a dictionary. A dispute about whether more people went to plays in England than in France would be terminated by making a survey and getting statistics. In the case of an argument between Croce and Bell, it seems to me that no appeal to facts, linguistic or about experiences, canvases, paints or anything else, would settle it to the satisfaction of both sides.

Croce is impressed by the role of the Imagination in creating and appreciating works of art; so he declares that Art *is* Intuition, something mentally created rather than painted, sculptured, or written. He is so impressed by this aspect that he regards the physical medium of a work of art as irrelevant. In this way his theory can be said to be prompted by an important æsthetic fact, but he so forms it that it transcends the facts until they can no longer count against it. He will not allow, for example, the importance most other people attach to the physical aspect of works of art to count against his view that they are purely non-physical. It becomes pointless to talk about 'refuting Croce's theory'. It can be valued, enjoyed, said to make an interesting point, but not factually refuted. For it is made in the *a priori* medium.

Clive Bell, on the other hand, is impressed by the value of formal relationships of line and colour in certain kinds of painting, Cézanne's, for example. He is so impressed by this aspect of a certain kind of art that he declares that 'Art is Significant Form'. This statement, too, arising from an æsthetic fact (namely, that in some works it is the formal designs that arouse æsthetic emotion) transcends the other facts about other sorts of art which go against it. Descriptive painting, for example, he declares to be 'not Art'. Although Bell claims to have isolated what is a common characteristic of all works of art, as someone might isolate alcohol as the common characteristic of all cocktails, what he has really done is to restrict the use of the word 'Art' to a certain sort of painting which seems to him very important and exciting. And of course it is impossible to refute someone who decides to restrict the meaning of a word. All we can do is sympathize with or regret his usage.

I conclude that very probably many conclusions in æsthetics are fabricated *a priori* statements, which originally arise from a desire to emphasize one fact about æsthetic objects and experience to the firm exclusion of the rest. A trivial example of the sort of statement I believe æsthetic statements to be like would be 'The only Universities in England are Oxford and Cambridge', made by a person who was so impressed by the virtues (and by none of the drawbacks) of the ancient universities that he is utterly unconvinced by having pointed out to him the facts which show that London, Liverpool, Manchester, etc., also have Universities. He has made 'The only Universities in England are Oxford and Cambridge' *a priori* true in so far as he refuses to say of any other educational institution in England that it is a 'University', refuses to admit any possible counter-instance. He has restricted the use of the phrase 'English University'. Such a person has said nothing interesting, valuable, or exciting, of course, but the parallel with the æsthetician who says that 'Art is such and such' is one of linguistic mechanism.

If what I believe about the nature of some æsthetic theories is correct, it is inappropriate to ask whether such theories are true or false, since they cannot be refuted empirically. It is inappropriate to point out counter-facts, since the theories are so stated that any such facts are impotent. It is only appropriate to sympathize with, or to feel opposed to, æsthetic theories, and to understand the artistic prejudices which have caused them.

CHAPTER VII

SOME DISTINCTIVE FEATURES OF ARGUMENTS USED IN CRITICISM OF THE ARTS

By *Margaret Macdonald*

[The original of this paper was the last of three in a Symposium in which the other two symposiasts were Mr. A. H. Hannay and Mr. John Holloway. The first part, therefore, contained references to their contributions. It has been impossible to delete these without completely destroying the original paper but they have been made as far as possible self-explanatory and footnote references added for those who wish to consult the original papers. I apologize to my fellow symposiasts. Part 2 has been expanded and partly re-written. I have not fundamentally altered the original doctrine but only tried to make clearer what I was trying to express in 1949. I no longer agree with all the views expressed in the paper. But I think it illustrates certain complexities in our use of the terms 'work of art' and 'æsthetically good' which are worth considering.—M. M.]

I

In his Preface Wordsworth says that he would not wish it to be supposed that he entertained the foolish hope of *reasoning* the reader into an approbation of the Lyrical Ballads. Certainly, it does seem queer to suppose that anyone could be *argued* into admiring *Persuasion* or condemning *The Stag at Eve*. This seems as absurd as to imagine that one could love and hate by argument. Yet the Preface increased the size of the volume by more than a score of pages. Whether or not this was argument, Wordsworth evidently did not regard it as a complete waste of time.

Works of art are esoteric objects.[1] That they hang on walls, together with cobwebs; stand on shelves, with aspidistras and cacti; are heard as are the noises of birds and trains, disguises their complexity. For they are not simple objects of sense perception. This may be less misleadingly expressed by saying that we do not use the term 'work of art' as simply equivalent to any terms describing physical objects and events. Those who listen to a concert, walk round a gallery, read a poem may have roughly

[1] Cf. also John Holloway, 'What are the distinctive features of arguments used in criticism of the arts?' (*Proc. Aris. Soc. Supp.* vol. XXIII, p. 173).

similar sense perceptions, but some get a great deal more than others from what is perceived and judge it differently. What is this 'something more', how is it acquired, and by what criterion is the subsequent judgment of value deemed to be right or wrong?

Wordsworth obviously thought that the Ballads might misfire and be received with indifference, amazement or contempt. He tried to forestall this reaction by some account of the poems and their production which should show that such a judgment would be hasty and ill-considered, if not wrong. He was writing as a critic and not as a poet. For critics attempt a certain kind of explanation of works of art with the object of establishing correct judgments of their artistic merit.

This kind of explanation of works of art may be distinguished from two others; those of scholarship and history. Scholarship establishes, *e.g.*, the original text of a literary, and the correct score of a musical, work. The scholar may, perhaps, without derogation, be compared to the expert picture cleaner. Both enable us to become acquainted with an original something instead of a begrimed and inaccurate substitute. The historian provides dates and other biographical and social information. We know as the result of these what was produced and why by a particular artist at a certain date. We still do not know its artistic value, *i.e.* whether and why it is a good specimen of its kind. To fill this gap is the task of the critic. The æsthetic problem is to elucidate what he does and how he does it. It is natural to assume that if disputation about art is not mere futile wrangling there must be some standards of appeal by which dispute may be terminated. Such standards are provided in logic by the principles of deductive inference; in science by scientific method and verifiable fact. These apply also in scholarship and history. The propositions of scholars and historians are about verifiable facts and are established by, or by something very like, the normal procedures of scientific method and logical argument. The question is whether there are comparable criteria in art criticism. No one seriously thinks that all judgments about art are of equal value. That critical procedures are admitted to differ from those of the establishment of facts is perhaps shown by the circumstance that Fleet Street employs political, sporting and scientific 'correspondents'; but literary, music, art, and dramatic 'critics'. Correspondents report facts; critics are evidently expected to perform a different task.

Some æsthetic philosophers, however, do seem to want to establish a criterion of agreement about critical conclusions in some procedures of reasoning and verification similar to those of deductive and inductive inference. Mr. A. H. Hannay, for example, has said,[1] 'behind individual criticisms of a work of art there always lies some general theory whether it is implicit or explicit'. I am puzzled about this use of 'theory'. It seems to assume that from observation of a selection of works of art, critics formulate hypotheses about a standard which all artists ought to achieve and by which their works may be judged. Further observation reveals contrary instances and the hypothesis is then superseded by an alternative. This is the familiar scientific procedure. But what sort of observation is relevant and what constitutes contrary instances, in art? Was Wordsworth establishing a contrary instance to the theory that all good poetry is written in a certain style? If so, it would seem, one must reject Milton and Pope in favour of Wordsworth and Coleridge as one rejects Newton in favour of Einstein. Or, perhaps, one should re-interpret the Augustan poets as 'limiting cases' of romanticism as Newton's theory may be re-interpreted as a limiting case of the more general theory of relativity. But this is surely wrong. Whatever the value of generalization in science, in art it invariably leads to sheer distortion. The scientist discovers new facts which refute the old theory or to which it must be adapted. Mr. Hannay seems to apply this procedure to Reynolds and the 'grand style'. He 'would question the validity of the reasons given by Reynolds for disparaging the Venetians',[2] presumably by showing that Venetian painting is good though it does not conform to Reynolds' criterion. It thus constitutes a contrary instance. He would reinforce his contention by showing Reynolds various causes why his opinion might be mere prejudice. But he does not indicate about precisely what Reynolds can be proved to be mistaken and prejudiced. The Aristotelian physicists who refused to look down Galileo's telescope rejected the new facts which would refute their theories. Since what is seen through telescopes is relevant to the truth of astronomical theories, they must be

[1] A. H. Hannay, loc. cit., p. 166.   [2] Loc. cit., p. 166.

condemned as prejudiced. But what new facts about the Venetians has Mr. Hannay discovered which Reynolds refused to admit? Roger Fry observes:

> Reynolds was so entirely at home in Venetian art; he felt its appeal so intensely, even basing upon it his own most magnificent designs and learning from it the secret of his rich and transparent colouring; that in the endeavour not to rate beyond its worth a style of which he was himself a master, he actually decried it more than justice required.[1]

It may be agreed that he did, but not, I suggest, from ignorance or prejudice. I doubt whether anyone could enlighten Reynolds on Venetian art. Yet he judged it inferior because not in the manner of Michael Angelo and Raphael. The Venetians were merely 'ornamental'. Mr. Hannay's disagreement with Reynolds seems to resolve itself into one not about facts or logic but nomenclature. This may not be trifling, but is quite different from disagreement about theory.

I think, however, that the view which Mr. Hannay wishes to oppose to that of Reynolds is that judgments of artistic merit are immediate responses to certain emotional states conveyed by artists in their work which we know from experience and can reproduce imaginatively in evaluating the work. Works of art are not judged by general rules as Reynolds supposed. To understand and check up on Reynolds' criticisms of Rigaud, for example, one must look at his portraits and 'try to repeat the imaginative process of the artist'.[2] The vulgarity of a piece of furniture is 'a process that we can observe and repeat in ourselves'.[3] We can recognize the laborious effort of George Eliot in producing the characters of *Daniel Deronda*. About these agreement is possible by something like an empirical test.

It would be foreign to the theme of this paper to discuss the thesis that works of art express emotional states. But it would be interesting to know by what criterion Mr. Hannay or anyone else could determine whether or not he had correctly reproduced the emotional state of any artist. What seems to me wrong in such a suggestion is that critical discussion conducts a factual investigation into the mental processes either of an artist or the members of his audience. For this seems to make criticism

---

[1] Reynolds, *Discourses*, ed. Roger Fry, 1905. Introduction to 4th Discourse.
[2] *Loc. cit.*, p. 167.   [3] *Ibid.*, p. 169.

just another exercise in empirical, including perhaps clinical, psychology. Do we really care whether a portrait painter feels genuine sentiment for his sitters? I don't believe we do or that it affects our judgment of his work. There is, however, no doubt that some critics do take this view. Certain critics of Shakespeare, for example, describe themselves as trying to discover 'what Shakespeare really meant'; 'what was in his mind'; 'what he was trying to express', etc. The temptation to say this is very understandable since such information might provide an objective standard of interpretation, if not of evaluation. For the problem of agreement about the interpretation of a work is often as acute as that about its merit. If one could know the state of mind in which a work was produced one could surely interpret it correctly. But this is an illusion. For a work of art is not a state of mind or the effect of such a state plus technical ability to handle a medium. However skilfully Shakespeare later described his mental state when writing *King Lear* this would not be the play he wrote. Nor are description and play the same thing in different words. This is obvious. One is about Shakespeare and the other about Lear and his daughters. Still less do we evaluate our own states of mind in judging a work of art or make them the criterion of its artistic merit. The critic's task is not to write his own or the artist's biography but to explain and evaluate a work of art.

Mr. John Holloway in his discussion of this subject[1] denies that criticism is a process of inferring a value judgment from the interpretation of a work of art. It is rather a technique to direct observation rightly, call attention to significant features, stimulate and develop æsthetic sensibility towards particular works. Critics do not formulate general standards and apply these mechanically to all, or to classes of, works of art. For every work of art is unique and in the last resort, perhaps, can be judged by no standards but its own. But, though unique, a work of art does not occur in isolation, but as part of bodies of similar works and within an artistic tradition. Throughout the history of an art there have accumulated a number of rules, prescriptions, prohibitions, called 'canons of the art'. A wise critic relates his spontaneous judgments to the wisdom distilled in these

[1] *Loc. cit.*, p. 175.

formulae though neither artist nor critic regards them as absolute norms. Indeed, their very existence may prove a challenge to defy or go beyond them. ('The Blue Boy' was Gainsborough's answer to one of Reynolds' strictures about colour.) Critical canons are more like rules of etiquette than morals and very unlike scientific laws or logical principles. They may be infringed and do not form a closed system. Nevertheless, they are of use in setting artistic problems and connecting critical judgments within a framework which discourages crankiness and partiality. The final standard, however, is the direct response to a work of art; the judgment of personal taste, and this may contravene all canons.

I should not quarrel with this as an account of much critical procedure. Mr. Holloway does not, however, examine its logical structure or estimate its value as a method of obtaining reliable judgments about works of art. He does not, for example, say whether the judgment of æsthetic value is an expression of certain feelings about the work or is of some other form. He observes that[1] 'The value judgment finds its proof, directly, in the object; but what validates it can be seen only by a sensitive observer whose attention is properly directed'. What is drawn attention to, however, does not, strictly, *prove* the value judgment, since this is not an inferred conclusion. But Mr. Holloway does not discuss whether the procedure is, alternatively, that of persuading to acceptance of the value judgment, or of some other type. I am also puzzled by this feature 'in the object' which can be seen only by a specially qualified observer. It is plain that a person who is tone deaf cannot appreciate Bach; that a blind man is bereft of the enjoyment of pictures. Perhaps only great stupidity or very narrow experience prevent the enjoyment of literary works. But Mr. Holloway is not concerned with these unfortunates. He assumes that criticism is addressed to those normally endowed with senses and understanding. He observes that critical, unlike ethical, discussion is designed to modify the sensibility of others. But what sort of endowment is this which talking can modify? What is its relation to features in an object of which we seem to be aware only by sense perception and understanding, *e.g.* colours, shapes, language and musical

[1] *Loc. cit.*, p. 175.

notation? Discussion does not improve eyesight and hearing, though it may assist understanding by giving new information or fresh ways of dealing with old information. But it is not quite clear what information is being given by the critic and how. Some philosophers have, of course, held that Taste is a special kind of sensation or flair possessed at least by some people. But how is this recognized apart from appreciating works of art? An affirmative answer to this might explain some of the disturbing differences in judgments about works of art. If some people are born philistines their views about art could be safely ignored. Like those of a blind man about pictures, they could only parrot those of the better endowed. Unfortunately, there seems no means of identifying these empty vessels. A rich experience of art, combined with critical reflection will generally improve æsthetic judgment. But this bears no resemblance to the sense in which a prolonged and discriminating experience of foods and drinks may literally modify an epicure's palate so that he can distinguish savours blurred or inaccessible to cruder tastes. It is, however, much less clear what kind of improvement occurs in æsthetic judgment.

Finally, this point is connected with the fallibility of all artistic canons. About a judgment in accordance with accepted canons there will generally be agreement among critics. But since canons have an 'open character' they will sometimes be contravened by a work of art or a critical judgment. The question then arises of what distinguishes a justified from an unjustified contravention. Mr. Holloway does not discuss this but he would probably agree that the decision is not simply one of personal preference. If only, however, it were a breach in favour of a feature discriminated by a special or more carefully trained sense its independence of mere whim or folly would be assured.

2

The logical type of value judgments affects the question whether critical discussion is argument to prove true and false propositions. I shall assume it to be generally agreed that value judgments are not simply descriptions of physical or psychological fact. For the statement that an object has certain physical qualities or an observer certain states is not an evaluation. 'This is good' does not *say* either 'This has certain observable qualities' or 'I admire this'. Nor shall I recapitulate the arguments against the view that judgments of æsthetic value assert the presence in an object of the non-natural quality 'æsthetic goodness' or 'beauty'. Moreover, while those who affirm value judgments take favourable or unfavourable attitudes to what is evaluated, value judgments seem to do more than express personal attitudes. They are 'objective' at least to the extent that those who agree or disagree with them do so without necessarily referring to any private feeling or sentiment. 'I admit that Raphael is a great painter but I do not like his work; it does not move me.' Such a statement is not self-contradictory, and very often true. If so, it is hard to believe that 'Raphael is a good painter' expresses a favourable attitude which the speaker denies. To suppose that he is expressing the attitude of no one in particular (if, indeed, this makes sense) is to remove the chief charm of the theory. 'This is good' is ostensibly similar to 'This is red'. If 'good' does not name a simple quality like 'red' then the sole alternative, it has been supposed, is that it names a simple feeling in the assertor. But 'This is good' also has the form of the impersonal verdict 'He is guilty' with which it may perhaps be more profitably compared. For a verdict does not describe the accused nor express the feelings of judge and jury. It affirms a decision reached by a definite procedure but unlike that of relating evidence to conclusion in deductive and inductive inference.[1] This is a situation which extends far beyond law courts, to show rings, examiners' meetings, selection boards. All these estimate qualifications and indicate a decision by certain signs, a prize, diploma, appointment. It is this activity, far more than those of logicians and scientists, which resembles the critic's. For he, too, adjudicates; he affirms merit or demerit. By calling a work 'good' he places the hall mark on an artistic performance. But he does not describe it or himself. So that to affirm a work good is more like bestowing a medal than naming any feature of it or of the states of its creators and audience. Verdicts and awards are not true or false. They may be reversed but not disproved.

[1] Cf. also J. Wisdom, 'Gods', *Logic and Language*, p. 187, and M. Macdonald, 'Natural Rights', *Proc. Aris. Soc.*, 1946–47, esp. pp. 242–50.

But they can be justified and unjustified. Both the verdict and the competence of the judges may be contested. The opposition protests that the verdict was wrong or unjust; not that it was false or invalid.

If this account is accepted then it follows that critical discussion cannot establish value judgments by deductive and inductive inference. They are neither deduced nor confirmed by empirical evidence. So no one, as Wordsworth said, can be *argued* into a favourable verdict on the Lyrical Ballads. Does it follow that such a verdict can be obtained only by graft, sales talk, wheedling or whatever other device will influence a capricious fancy? No, for though these may obtain, they do not *justify*, a decision. The word 'judge' does not properly apply to those, like the Duchess in *Alice in Wonderland*, who indulge a liking for cutting off heads. Nor to those, more amiable, like the Dodo, who give prizes to everyone. Even a bad judge makes some pretence of observing a procedure other than mere caprice. So, too, a critic is worthy of the name only if he distributes verdicts with discrimination. But discrimination about what, and what sort of procedure justifies a value judgment about art? What sort of considerations are invoked, and how, to justify a critical verdict?

I have said that we ordinarily distinguish a work of art from a physical object. That we use these terms differently. 'That', exclaims A triumphantly, pointing to his newly acquired canvas, 'is a great picture!' 'I should not call it a picture', retorts B, 'but only a pot of paint flung in the face of a gullible public!'[1] It seems clear that both have located the same physical object but that not both have located a work of art. Nor will it be of much use to tell B to look more closely and carefully when he will find the work of art hidden in the paint, like the monkey in the branches of a child's puzzle. He may look as hard as you please, but he will not succeed, for in *that* sense there is nothing more to find. It is not perceptual tricks which distinguish a painted canvas from a work of art. Remember Reynolds and the Venetians. What B lacks is not observation but that which A must supply as a critic to support his judgment, instruction, and interpretation. The distinction between physical object and work of art is even more complicated for the non-plastic arts. Even if

---

[1] Cf. Ruskin *v.* Whistler.

one *can* locate 'Cremorne Lights' on the wall of a certain room in the National Gallery, where can one locate Shakespeare's plays or Beethoven's symphonies? I have an object on my bookshelf, of the same type as the shelf, a copy of Shakespeare's Works; I have the score and a set of records of a Beethoven symphony. So have thousands of others, and they have the same works. When I talk of these works I do not refer only to my particular copies. But by 'Cremorne Lights' I mean the original by Whistler in the National Gallery of which anything resembling it is a mere copy and *not* the same work. The type/token distinction applies to literary and musical but not to works of the plastic arts. I do not propose to discuss this further except to say that it shows that while a work of the plastic arts cannot, logically, be in more than one place at one time, this is not true of literary and musical works. Hence it is much more plausible to suppose that in painting and sculpture one refers simply to a physical object when talking of a work of art. But this is not true of any works of art. Because it is not, certain idealist æsthetic philosophers, *e.g.* Croce[1] and Collingwood,[2] have held that a work of art is a mental image, an imaginary or 'ideal' object for which its physical expression in words, paint, stone, sounds, etc., is a mere vehicle, a stimulus to the reproduction of the 'real' work in an observer's mind. For Alexander[3] the work of art is a material thing magically endowed with mysterious life by the artist and so turned into an illusion, though a beautiful illusion. For Sartre, too, the work of art is 'something unreal' for which the artist constructs a material analogue in the external world.[4] There is obviously a very strong temptation to treat the work of art as a mysterious entity, somewhat like a genie in its physical bottle. But if a work of art is not a physical object, it does not follow that it is a mental state or ghost. These do not exhaust the possibilities for not all discourse which uses substantival words and phrases need be 'about' objects. If one wished to be metaphysically paradoxical one might say that a

---

[1] *Æsthetic*, trans. D. Ainslie. London, Macmillan, 1922.
[2] *Principles of Art.* Oxford University Press, 1938.
[3] Cf. *Beauty and other Forms of Value.* London, Macmillan, 1933; also Paul Ziff on 'Art and the "Object of Art" ', this volume, p. 170.
[4] *The Psychology of Imagination*, trans. New York, Philosophical Library, 1948. Conclusion, Section 2, 'The Work of Art'.

I

work of art is not an object of any sort but only, as it were, a manner of speaking, though this, of course, is also highly misleading if taken seriously. But æsthetic, like all other philosophical problems, are those of how words are used rather than of what kinds of objects exist.

The problem of how 'work of art' is used, which I confess I cannot satisfactorily solve and may even be wrong in considering a problem, does at present seem to me connected with the question of how value judgments in art are justified and hence with that of critical interpretation. 'Work of art' is a cultural, not an everyday term. Like 'electron' its use is learned by a more sophisticated process than that of 'table'. Someone may object that this is only because 'work of art' is a general term and these should be avoided in philosophy. Everyone knows the difference between a poem, a play, a picture, a statue, a symphony. These are 'works of art' so why so much fuss? I can only say that even in particular cases there sometimes seems to be difficulty about what is being discussed and evaluated in art.

I shall introduce my difficulties by referring to some points in Mrs. Helen Knight's discussion of 'The Use of "Good" in Æsthetic Judgments'.[1] Mrs. Knight compares the use of 'good' in '*Persuasion* is a good novel', 'Cézanne's "Green Jar" is a good picture' with its use in such judgments as ' "Serena" is a good Persian cat', ' "Lady Jane" is a good arum lily', 'Joan is a good knitter', etc. The similarity in all such uses is the existence of a set of criteria-qualities for good novels, good Persian cats, good knitters, etc., which, when indicated, justify the use of 'good' for each type of performance. Works of art may be good for many such 'reasons'. There are many different criteria of merit recognized by critics. They form an indefinite and increasing family. Their exemplification can, however, be recognized in particular works of art which may be judged accordingly.

Mrs. Knight's interesting account does not quite satisfy me, for two reasons. (1) Two Persian cats, two tennis players, two roses, two knitters, may tie for first place. There may be 'nothing to choose between them'. They exemplify the agreed criteria-characters to an indistinguishable degree. But I am not sure that it makes sense to say that *Emma* and *Persuasion* might compete

---

[1] See this volume, pp. 147–60.

for the same place; that two works, even by the same artist, might excel by exhibiting certain meritorious characters in a way which makes them qualitatively indistinguishable. There could be twin prize cats, but it seems to me logically impossible that there should be twin masterpieces in art. Works of art are unique. Their performance cannot be repeated even by the artist. In this they seem to differ from certain other performances in which what is produced, though numerically different, may be qualitatively exactly similar. This is not a mysterious natural fact, but simply a characteristic of the way in which we talk about works of art. No doubt the borrower from a circulating library who just wants a 'good' novel for the week-end will accept any standard work. But then he is not interested in art. For those who are, though *The Portrait of a Lady* has much in common with *The Wings of the Dove* and both are good novels, it would seem absurd to list their characteristics and suppose them to add up to the same sum. One would not be content to lose either so long as the other were retained. They are not simply substitutable for each other. This would be admitted by any competent critic. (2) My second objection to Mrs. Knight's account is that it seems to assume that a work of art is an object rather like a cake, whose meritorious features may be picked out, like plums, and exhibited. The model suggested to me is of a combination of ingredients which it is the business of the critic to exhibit to justify his approval of the work. There is, *e.g.*, one object, the play of *Hamlet*, whose features can be revealed once and for all by expert interpretation and the result evaluated. Mrs. Knight gives an example of this in the description of its characters by which she would support a favourable verdict on Cézanne's 'Green Jar'.[1]

If this is the correct story, it is strange that the task of interpreting and evaluating a work of art seems to be never completed. In art, the dead are never finally buried. The re-interpreting and revaluating of established, and the resurrecting of forgotten, works is a favourite activity of critics. One need only think of the procession of critics of Shakespeare. Yet many of them from Johnson to the latest name may still be read with profit. Is it because the features of Shakespeare's plays are so

[1] *Loc. cit.*, p. 152.

inexhaustible that no one critic can ever finally list them as adequate grounds for value judgments? Or is it because the plays are not simple objects whose features can be presented for listing? To suppose that they are is, again, to be misled by the methods of science. Scientists observe and explain the behaviour of objects. Whether bodies are observed to fall by X in Italy in the sixteenth century or by Y in London in the twentieth does not affect the result, unless new facts are relevant. I have suggested that new facts in this sense about works of art are discovered only by scholars and historians whose methods are scientific. There are few such facts about Shakespeare's plays known to-day which were unknown to Dr. Johnson, though later interpretations of the plays and perhaps their evaluation have differed. It is often said that a great artist is reinterpreted in every age and no doubt by some of these interpretations he would be much astonished. Yet even the apparently bizarre interpretations are often illuminating. It seems to follow that interpretation is partly subjective invention, but about this there could be endless argument of the sort that would hardly be necessary about the description of a chair or horse, except perhaps in extreme border-line cases. Certainly, the critic claims to be interpreting the work, not supplying his own fancies. But the work is what it is interpreted to be, though some interpretations may be rejected. There seems to be no work apart from *some* interpretation.

This critical function may be illustrated by another form of interpretation. The presentation of the character of 'Hamlet' by actors from Richard Burbage to John Gielgud is of 'the same character'. Each actor impersonates 'Hamlet' and speaks the lines given in any text of the play. Yet the effect of each interpretation may be very different but, apart from presentation through someone, what is *the* character 'Hamlet'? Does each actor find something in 'Hamlet' missed by the rest or is it not rather that the character is a construction from this series of interpretations upon a text and evaluated by means of its members? Music and its executants are another example of interpretations which seem to constitute a work of art. A musical work is composed for performance but each performance while playing the notes of the same score varies, often widely, from any other. A great conductor, with a responsive orchestra, may give an entirely fresh meaning to a hackneyed composition. Yet, again, the composition does not exist as a *musical* work apart from some performance. It is a construction from such performances. Nor need such performances be actual. In reading *Hamlet* or following a score one imagines a performance, gives a certain interpretation to the words and notes even though this may be a very poor relation of that given by a great actor or executant. The point is that there is no object which is 'the real' play or sonata which exists independently of any interpretation. If it be said that there is such an object, *viz*. the play or sonata as it existed in the minds of Shakespeare or Mozart, then the reply must surely be that if this is so we must remain not only ignorant of, but literally *without* these works, since we cannot restore the dead. I do not think we are condemned to such a pessimistic conclusion. Nor does this view conflict with the statement that a work of art is unique. For the fact that there could not be another play of exactly the same merit as *Hamlet* is not incompatible with its construction from many interpretations. This is an attempt to explain what is meant when we say that there is such a play, or any work of art.

I suggest that the task of the critic resembles those of the actor and executant rather than those of the scientist and logician. Another fruitful comparison might be with that of a good Counsel. The Counsel, too, has the 'facts' but from them he 'creates' his client's case. So the critic must present what is not obvious to casual or uninstructed inspection, *viz*. a work of art. Of course, he is not to be identified with an actor, executant or Counsel. He differs from these in one very important respect, in being also a judge of what he presents. That a critic is 'creative' is not very revolutionary doctrine and most great critics have been great showmen of their subjects. Such were Ruskin on Turner, Clive Bell and Roger Fry on Cézanne and the Post-Impressionists, Coleridge on Shakespeare and, finally, Wordsworth on the Lyrical Ballads. Should we have the works we value, without these and other advocates? But to a lesser degree we are all critics in relation to art. Some construction must precede serious judgment.

To judge a work of art, therefore, is to give a verdict on something to which the judge has contributed and this also 'justifies' the verdict. It is an odd sort of justification, perhaps more like that by which we try to 'justify' our affections and antipathies. For a work of art appeals to more than the intellect. People often develop for their favourite works an almost personal relationship for which 'reasons' seem irrelevant. This should not be exaggerated, but is an element in the attitude to art which makes an account of 'proving' a value judgment by the listing of criteria-characters seem inappropriately mechanical. Not in that way, one protests, is conviction induced.

But if each interpretation is individual how is one to explain the fact that different ages or even different persons in any age evaluate the 'same' work of art? One might suggest that 'same' here is used analogously to its use in 'same function' and *Hamlet* is a function of which individual interpretations are values as '*x* is a man' is a function of which individual men are values. Of course, they are not exactly similar for *Hamlet* is not a universal or set of universals of which its interpretations are instances as 'Man' is a universal of which individual men are instances. My reading of *Hamlet* is not an 'instance' of *Hamlet* though it is one of a vast number of more or less similar performances without which, I suggest, it would make no sense to speak of the play. The idea of a 'work of art-in-itself' which can never conceivably be experienced is as mythical as a 'material object-in-itself' which can never conceivably be perceived. But neither are its interpretations connected in the construction of a work of art as sense data are connected in the construction of a physical object on the phenomenalist thesis. If the work of art is such a construction as I have suggested, it is unique and not to be identified with any others with which it may be compared. The history of the arts, of criticism and evaluation, does seem to show that 'work of art' is not used for simple, identifiable objects which can be indicated like a pebble on a beach or a book on a shelf, but rather for something like a set of variations on a basic theme.

I wonder whether æsthetic philosophers do not make too much fuss about 'sameness' and 'objectivity' in art. Art is different from morals. It may be important that for Shakespeare as for us stealing a purse is theft, and wrong; wrong, perhaps, for all rational beings who acknowledge private property. I am much less sure that the play which Shakespeare's audience enjoyed as *Hamlet* is identical with that enjoyed now. Not only in matters such as text, which scholarship can rectify, but as a work of art. Since our circumstances and background are utterly different from those of the first Elizabethans, such an identity seems most unlikely. A simple, but important, difference is that the work would have *sounded* very different in Elizabethan English. As different as Bach's music would sound on the instruments for which it was originally composed. If we and our ancestors could change places each might loathe the other's version and we might wrangle interminably about which was the 'real' work. The answer is, surely, *both* and that there are and will continue to be innumerable members of the family. This may also be part of the answer to our differences with Reynolds about the Venetians. The problem becomes one of choosing an emphasis: same work but *different versions*; different versions but the *same work*. Either alternative is valid.

So, to affirm that a work of art is good or bad is to commend or condemn, but not describe. To justify such a verdict is not to give general criteria as 'reasons' but to 'convey' the work as a pianist might 'show' the value of a sonata by playing it. Critical talk about a work is, as it were, a construction of it by someone at a particular time, in a certain social context. Thus criticism does not, and cannot, have the impersonal character and strict rules, applicable independently of time and place, appropriate to science and mathematics. A mathematician who claimed to have squared the circle, a scientist who announced a law for which he could give no empirical evidence, would be justly ridiculed. But to attempt to legislate for art is to invite successful infringement of any law, as the 'Unities' showed. Criticism is, therefore, I suggest, an indefinite set of devices for 'presenting' not 'proving' the merits of works of art. It has none of the stability of logical truth, scientific method, legal and moral law. It varies with time, place and audience, while not being completely subject to these limitations. For it is certainly possible to appreciate the work of artists and critics of other ages and cultures. But the differences are as important as any common characters and must be equally respected. It is mythical to suppose that one can distil some 'eternal essences' which are works of art and some uniform method of their appraisal from the vast and complex system of relationships between artists and their audiences throughout the history of art. Art is creation, not discovery. Criticism and appraisal, too, are more like creation than like demonstration and proof.

Does it follow from this that all judgments about art are of equal value, which I began by denying? I do not think so. But they are not measured by correspondence with the qualities of some mythical object, the 'real work of art' independent of all interpretation. Instead, they are generally appraised in relation to qualities of the critic. The judgments of a skilful, sympathetic, widely experienced critic are better than those of one without these, and other appropriate qualities. But 'better' and 'worse' judgments are probably all that can be achieved in this field. No critic, even the best, is infallible and sometimes we may be well advised to trust our own judgment rather than that of any expert.

CHAPTER VIII

CRITICAL COMMUNICATION[1]

By *Arnold Isenberg*

THAT questions about meaning are provisionally separable, even if finally inseparable, from questions about validity and truth, is shown by the fact that meanings can be exchanged without the corresponding cognitive decisions. What is imparted by one person to another in an act of communication is (typically) a certain idea, thought, content, meaning, or claim—not a belief, expectation, surmise, or doubt; for the last are dependent on factors, such as the checking process, which go beyond the mere understanding of the message conveyed. And there is a host of questions which have to do with this message: its simplicity or complexity, its clarity or obscurity, its tense, its mood, its modality, and so on. Now, the theory of art criticism has, I think, been seriously hampered by a kind of headlong assault on the question of validity. We have many doctrines about the objectivity of the critical judgment but few concerning its import, or claim to objectivity, though the settlement of the first of these questions probably depends on the clarification of the second. The following remarks are for the most part restricted to meeting such questions as: What is the content of the critic's argument? What claim does he transmit to us? How does he expect us to deal with this claim?

A good point to start from is a theory of criticism, widely held in spite of its deficiencies, which divides the critical process into three parts. There is the value judgment or *verdict* (V): 'This picture or poem is good—'. There is a particular statement or *reason* (R): '—because it has such-and-such a quality—'. And there is a general statement or *norm* (N): '—and any work which has that quality is *pro tanto* good'.[2]

model

---

[1] The author is indebted to Mr. Herbert Bohnert for assistance with this paper.

[2] Cf., for instance, C. J. Ducasse, *Art, the Critics, and You* (p. 116): 'The statement that a given work possesses a certain objective characteristic expresses at the same time a judgment of value if the characteristic is one that the judging person approves or, as the case may be, disapproves; and is thus one that he regards as conferring, respectively, positive or negative value on any object of the given kind that happens to possess it' See, further, pp. 117–20.

V has been construed, and will be construed here, as an expression of feeling—an utterance manifesting praise or blame. But among utterances of that class it is distinguished by being in some sense conditional upon R. This is only another phrasing of the commonly noted peculiarity of æsthetic feeling: that it is 'embodied' in or 'attached' to an æsthetic content.

R is a statement describing the content of an art work; but not every such descriptive statement will be a case of R. The proposition, 'There are just twelve flowers in that picture' (and with it nine out of ten descriptions in Crowe and Cavalcaselle), is without critical relevance; that is, without any bearing upon V. The description of a work of art is seldom attempted for its own sake. It is controlled by some purpose, some interest; and there are many interests by which it might be controlled other than that of reaching or defending a critical judgment. The qualities which are significant in relation to one purpose—dating, attribution, archæological reconstruction, clinical diagnosis, proving or illustrating some thesis in sociology—might be quite immaterial in relation to another. At the same time, we cannot be sure that there is any *kind* of statement about art, serving no matter what main interest, which cannot also act as R; or, in other words, that there is any *kind* of knowledge about art which cannot influence æsthetic appreciation.

V and R, it should be said, are often combined in sentences which are at once normative and descriptive. If we have been told that the colours of a certain painting are garish, it would be astonishing to find that they were all very pale and unsaturated; and to this extent the critical comment conveys information. On the other hand, we might find the colours bright and intense, as expected, without being thereby forced to admit that they are garish; and this reveals the component of valuation (that is, distaste) in the critic's remark. This feature of critical usage has attracted much notice and some study; but we do not discuss it here at all. We shall be concerned solely with the descriptive function of R.

Now if we ask what makes a description critically useful and relevant, the first suggestion which occurs is that it is *supported by N*. N is based upon an inductive generalization which describes a relationship between some æsthetic quality and someone's or everyone's system of æsthetic response. Notice: I do not say that N *is* an inductive generalization; for in critical evaluation N is being used not to predict or to explain anybody's reaction to a work of art but to vindicate that reaction, perhaps to someone who does not yet share it; and in this capacity N is a precept, a rule, a *generalized value statement.* But the *choice* of one norm, rather than another, when that choice is challenged, will usually be given some sort of inductive justification. We return to this question in a moment. I think we shall find that a careful analysis of N is unnecessary, because there are considerations which permit us to dismiss it altogether.

At this point it is well to remind ourselves that there is a difference between *explaining* and *justifying* a critical response. A psychologist who should be asked 'why X likes the object y' would take X's enjoyment as a datum, a fact to be explained. And if he offers as explanation the presence in y of the quality Q, there is, explicit or latent in this causal argument, an appeal to some generalization which he has reason to think is true, such as 'X likes any work which has that quality'. But when we ask X as a critic 'why he likes the object y', we want him to give us some reason to like it too and are not concerned with the causes of what we may so far regard as his bad taste. This distinction between genetic and normative inquiry, though it is familiar to all and acceptable to most of us, is commonly ignored in the practice of æsthetic speculation; and the chief reason for this—other than the ambiguity of the question 'Why do you like this work?'—is the fact that some statements about the object will necessarily figure both in the explanation and in the critical defence of any reaction to it. Thus, if I tried to explain my feeling for the line

But musical as is Apollo's lute,

I should certainly mention 'the pattern of u's and l's which reinforces the meaning with its own musical quality'; for this quality of my sensations is doubtless among the conditions of my feeling response. And the same point would be made in any effort to convince another person of the beauty of the line. The remark which gives a reason also, in this case, states a cause. But notice that, though as criticism this comment might be very effective, it is practically worthless as explanation; for we have no phonetic

or psychological laws (nor any plausible 'common-sense'
generalizations) from which we might derive the prediction that
such a pattern of u's and l's should be pleasing to me. In fact,
the formulation ('pattern of u's and l's', etc.) is so vague that one
could not tell just what general hypothesis it is that is being
invoked or assumed; yet it is quite sharp enough for critical
purposes. On the other hand, suppose that someone should fail
to be 'convinced' by my argument in favour of Milton's line.
He might still readily admit that the quality of which I have
spoken might have something to do with *my* pleasurable reaction,
given my peculiar mentality. Thus the statement which is
serving both to explain and to justify is not equally effective
in the two capacities; and this brings out the difference between
the two lines of argument. Coincident at the start, they diverge
in the later stages. A *complete* explanation of any of my responses
would have to include certain propositions about my nervous
system, which would be irrelevant in any critical argument.
And a critically relevant observation about some configuration
in the art object might be useless for explaining a given experience,
if only because the experience did not yet contain that configuration.[1]

Now it would not be strange if, among the dangers of
ambiguity to which the description of art, like the rest of human
speech, is exposed, there should be some which derive from
the double purpose—critical and psychological—to which such
description is often being put. And this is, as we shall see, the
case.

The necessity for sound inductive generalizations in any attempt
at æsthetic explanation is granted. We may now consider, very
briefly, the parallel role in normative criticism which has been
assigned to N. Let us limit our attention to those metacritical
theories which *deny* a function in criticism to N. I divide these

---

[1] I should like to add that when we speak of 'justifying' or 'giving reasons' for our
critical judgments, we refer to something which patently does go on in the world and
which is patently different from the causal explanation of tastes and preferences. We are
not begging any question as to whether the critical judgment can 'really' be justified; that
is, established on an objective basis. Even if there were no truth or falsity in criticism, there
would still be agreement and disagreement; and there would be argument which arises out
of disagreement and attempts to resolve it. Hence, at the least there exists the purely
'phenomenological' task of elucidating the import and intention of words like 'insight',
'acumen', 'obtuseness', 'bad taste', all of which have a real currency in criticism.

into two kinds, those which attack existing standards and those which attack the very notion of a critical standard.

(1) It is said that we know of no law which governs human tastes and preferences, no quality shared by any two works of art that makes those works attractive or repellent. The point might be debated; but it is more important to notice what it assumes. It assumes that if N *were* based on a sound induction, it would be (together with R) a real ground for the acceptance of V. In other words, it would be reasonable to accept V on the strength of the quality Q if it could be shown that works which possess Q tend to be pleasing. It follows that criticism is being held back by the miserable state of æsthetic science. This raises an issue too large to be canvassed here. Most of us believe that the idea of progress applies to science, does not apply to art, applies, in some unusual and not very clear sense, to philosophy. What about criticism? Are there 'discoveries' and 'contributions' in this branch of thought? Is it reasonable to expect better evaluations of art after a thousand years of criticism than before? The question is not a simple one: it admits of different answers on different interpretations. But I do think that some critical judgments have been and are every day being 'proved' as well as in the nature of the case they ever can be proved. I think we have already numerous passages which are not to be corrected or improved upon. And if this opinion is right, then it could not be the case that the validation of critical judgments waits upon the discovery of aesthetic laws. Let us suppose even that we *had* some law which stated that a certain colour combination, a certain melodic sequence, a certain type of dramatic hero has everywhere and always a positive emotional effect. To the extent to which this law holds, there is of course that much less disagreement in criticism; but there is no better method for resolving disagreement. We are not more fully convinced in our own judgment because we know its explanation; and we cannot hope to convince an imaginary opponent by appeal to this explanation, which by hypothesis does not hold for him.

(2) The more radical arguments against critical standards are spread out in the pages of Croce, Dewey, Richards, Prall, and the great romantic critics before them. They need not be repeated here. In one way or another they all attempt to expose

the absurdity of presuming to judge a work of art, the very excuse for whose existence lies in its *difference* from everything that has gone before, by its degree of *resemblance* to something that has gone before; and on close inspection they create at least a very strong doubt as to whether a standard of success or failure in art is either necessary or possible. But it seems to me that they fail to provide a positive interpretation of criticism. Consider the following remarks by William James on the criticism of Herbert Spencer: 'In all his dealings with the art products of mankind he manifests the same curious dryness and mechanical literality of judgment. . . . Turner's painting he finds untrue in that the earth-region is habitually as bright in tone as the air-region. Moreover, Turner scatters his detail too evenly. In Greek statues the hair is falsely treated. Renaissance painting is spoiled by unreal illumination. Venetian Gothic sins by meaningless ornamentation.' And so on. We should most of us agree with James that this is bad criticism. But *all* criticism is similar to this in that it cites, as reasons for praising or condemning a work, one or more of its qualities. If Spencer's reasons are descriptively true, how can we frame our objection to them except in some such terms as that 'unreal illumination does not make a picture bad'; that is, by attacking his standards? What constitutes the relevance of a reason but its correlation with a norm? It is astonishing to notice how many writers, formally committed to an opposition to legal procedure in criticism, *seem* to relapse into a reliance upon standards whenever they give reasons for their critical judgments. The appearance is inevitable; for as long as we have no alternative interpretation of the import and function of R, we must assume *either* that R is perfectly arbitrary *or* that it presupposes and depends on some general claim.

   With these preliminaries, we can examine a passage of criticism. This is Ludwig Goldscheider on *The Burial of Count Orgaz*:

> Like the contour of a violently rising and falling wave is the outline of the four illuminated figures in the foreground: steeply upwards and downwards about the grey monk on the left, in mutually inclined curves about the yellow of the two saints, and again steeply upwards and downwards about . . . the priest on the right. The depth of the wave indicates the optical centre; the double curve of the saints' yellow garments is carried by the greyish white of

the shroud down still farther; in this lowest depth rests the bluish-grey armour of the knight.

This passage—which, we may suppose, was written to justify a favourable judgment on the painting—conveys to us the idea of a certain quality which, if we believe the critic, we should expect to find in a certain painting by El Greco. And we do find it: we can verify its presence by perception. In other words, there is a quality in the picture which agrees with the quality which we 'have in mind'—which we have been led to think of by the critic's language. But the same quality ('a steeply rising and falling curve', etc.) would be found in any of a hundred lines one could draw on the board in three minutes. It could not be the critic's purpose to inform us of the presence of a quality as obvious as this. It seems reasonable to suppose that the critic is thinking of another quality, no idea of which is transmitted to us by his language, which he *sees* and which by his use of language he *gets us to see*. This quality is, of course, a wavelike contour; but it is not the quality designated by the *expression* 'wavelike contour'. Any object which has this quality will have a wavelike contour; but it is not true that any object which has a wavelike contour will have this quality. At the same time, the expression 'wavelike contour' *excludes* a great many things: if anything is a wavelike contour, it is not a colour, it is not a mass, it is not a straight line. Now the critic, besides imparting to us the idea of a wavelike contour, gives us directions for perceiving, and does this *by means* of the idea he imparts to us, which narrows down the field of possible visual orientations and guides us in the discrimination of details, the organization of parts, the grouping of discrete objects into patterns. It is as if we found both an oyster and a pearl when we had been looking for a sea-shell because we had been told it was valuable. It *is* valuable, but not because it is a seashell.

I may be stretching usage by the senses I am about to assign to certain words, but it seems that the critic's *meaning* is 'filled in', 'rounded out', or 'completed' by the act of perception, which is performed not to judge the truth of his description but in a certain sense to *understand* it. And if *communication* is a process by which a mental content is transmitted by symbols from one person to another, then we can say that it is a function of criticism to bring about communication at the level of the senses; that is, to induce a sameness of vision, of experienced content. If this is accomplished, it may or may not be followed by agreement, or what is called 'communion'—a community of feeling which expresses itself in identical value judgments.

There is a contrast, therefore, between critical communication and what I may call normal or ordinary communication. In ordinary communication, symbols tend to acquire a footing relatively independent of sense-perception. It is, of course, doubtful whether the interpretation of symbols is at any time completely unaffected by the environmental context. But there is a difference of degree between, say, an exchange of glances which, though it means 'Shall we go home?' at one time and place, would mean something very different at another— between this and formal science, whose vocabulary and syntax have relatively fixed connotations. With a passage of scientific prose before us, we may be dependent on experience for the definition of certain simple terms, as also for the confirmation of assertions; but we are not dependent on experience for the interpretation of compound expressions. If we are, this exposes semantical defects in the passage—obscurity, vagueness, ambiguity, or incompleteness. (Thus: 'Paranoia is marked by a profound egocentricity and deep-seated feelings of insecurity'— the kind of remark which makes every student think he has the disease—is suitable for easy comparison of notes among clinicians, who know how to recognize the difference between paranoia and other conditions; but it does not explicitly set forth the criteria which they employ.) Statements about immediate experience, made in ordinary communication, are no exception. If a theory requires that a certain flame should be blue, then we have to report whether it is or is not blue—regardless of shades or variations which may be of enormous importance æsthetically. We are bound to the letters of our words. Compare with this something like the following:

'The expression on her face was delightful.'

'What was delightful about it?'

'Didn't you see that smile?'

The speaker does not mean that there is something delightful about smiles as such; but he cannot be accused of not stating his meaning clearly, because the clarity of his language must be judged in relation to his purpose, which in this case is the *evaluation* of the immediate experience; and for that purpose the reference to the smile will be sufficient if it gets people to feel that they are 'talking about the same thing'. There is understanding and misunderstanding at this level; there are marks by which the existence of one or the other can be known; and there are means by which misunderstanding can be eliminated. But these phenomena are not identical with those that take the same names in the study of ordinary communication.

Reading criticism, otherwise than in the presence, or with direct recollection, of the objects discussed is a blank and senseless employment—a fact which is concealed from us by the co-operation, in our reading, of many non-critical purposes for which the information offered by the critic is material and useful. There is not in all the world's criticism a single purely descriptive statement concerning which one is prepared to say beforehand, 'If it is true, I shall like that work so much the better'—and *this* fact is concealed by the play of memory, which gives the critic's language a quite different, more specific, meaning than it has as ordinary communication. The point is not at all similar to that made by writers who maintain that value judgments have no objective basis because the reasons given to support them are not logically derivable from the value judgments themselves. I do not ask that R be related *logically* to V. In ethical argument you have someone say, 'Yes, I would condemn that policy if it really did cause a wave of suicides, as you maintain'. Suppose that the two clauses are here only psychologically related—still, this is what you never have in criticism. *The truth of R never adds the slightest weight to V*, because R does not designate any quality the perception of which might induce us to assent to V. But if it is not R, or what it designates, that makes V acceptable, then R cannot possibly require the support of N. The critic is not committed to the general claim that the quality named Q is valuable because he never makes the particular claim that a work is good in virtue of the presence of Q.

But he, or his readers, can easily be misled into *thinking* that he has made such a claim. You have, perhaps, a conflict of opinion about the merits of a poem; and one writer defends his

K

judgment by mentioning vowel sounds, metrical variations, consistent or inconsistent imagery. Another critic, taking this language at its face value in ordinary communication, points out that 'by those standards' one would have to condemn famous passages in *Hamlet* or *Lear* and raise some admittedly bad poems to a high place. He may even attempt what he calls an 'experiment' and, to show that his opponents' grounds are irrelevant, construct a travesty of the original poem in which its plot or its meter or its vowels and consonants, or whatever other qualities have been cited with approval, are held constant while the rest of the work is changed. This procedure, which takes up hundreds of the pages of our best modern critics, is a waste of time and space; for it is the critic abandoning his own function to pose as a scientist—to assume, in other words, that criticism explains experiences instead of clarifying and altering them. If he saw that the *meaning* of a word like 'assonance'—the quality which it leads our perception to discriminate in one poem or another— is in critical usage never twice the same, he would see no point in 'testing' any generalization about the relationship between assonance and poetic value.

Some of the foregoing remarks will have reminded you of certain doctrines with which they were not intended to agree. The fact that criticism does not actually designate the qualities to which it somehow directs our attention has been a ground of complaint by some writers, who tell us that our present critical vocabulary is woefully inadequate.[1] This proposition clearly looks to an eventual improvement in the language of criticism. The same point, in a stronger form and with a different moral, is familiar to readers of Bergson and Croce, who say that it is impossible by means of concepts to 'grasp the essence' of the artistic fact; and this position has seemed to many people to display the ultimate futility of critical analysis. I think that by returning to the passage I quoted from Goldscheider about the painting by El Greco we can differentiate the present point of view from both of these. Imagine, then, that the painting should be projected on to a graph with intersecting co-ordinates. It would then be possible to write complicated mathematical expressions which would enable another person who knew the system

---

[1] See D. W. Prall, *Æsthetic Analysis*, p. 201.

to construct for himself as close an approximation to the exact outlines of the El Greco as we might desire. Would this be an advance towards precision in criticism? Could we say that we had devised a more specific terminology for drawing and painting? I think not, for the most refined concept remains a concept; there is no vanishing point at which it becomes a percept. It is the idea *of* a quality, it is not the quality itself. To render a critical verdict we should still have to perceive the quality; but Goldscheider's passage already shows it to us as clearly as language can. The idea of a new and better means of communication presupposes the absence of the sensory contents we are talking about; but criticism always assumes the presence of these contents to both parties; and it is upon this assumption that the vagueness or precision of a critical statement must be judged. Any further illustration of this point will have to be rough and hasty. For the last twenty or thirty years the 'correct' thing to say about the metaphysical poets has been this: They think with their senses and feel with their brains. One hardly knows how to verify such a dictum: as a psychological observation it is exceedingly obscure. But it does not follow that it is not acute criticism; for it increases our awareness of the difference between Tennyson and Donne. Many words—like 'subtlety', 'variety', 'complexity', 'intensity'—which in ordinary communication are among the vaguest in the language have been used to convey sharp critical perceptions. And many expressions which have a clear independent meaning are vague and fuzzy when taken in relation to the content of a work of art. An examination of the ways in which the language of concepts mediates between perception and perception is clearly called for, though it is far too difficult to be attempted here.

We have also just seen reason to doubt that any æsthetic quality is ultimately ineffable. 'What can be said' and 'what cannot be said' are phrases which take their meaning from the purpose for which we are speaking. The æsthetics of obscurantism, in its insistence upon the incommunicability of the art object, has never made it clear what purpose or demand is to be served by communication. If we devised a system of concepts by which a work of art could be virtually reproduced at a distance by the use of language alone, what human intention would be furthered? We

saw that *criticism* would not be improved: in the way in which
criticism strives to 'grasp' the work of art, we could grasp it no
better then than now. The scientific *explanation* of aesthetic
experiences would not be accomplished by a mere change
of descriptive terminology. There remains only the *æsthetic*
motive in talking about art. Now if we set it up as a condition
of communicability that our language should *afford* the experience
which it purports to describe, we shall of course reach the conclusion that art is incommunicable. But by that criterion all
reality is unintelligible and ineffable, just as Bergson maintains.
Such a demand upon thought and language is not only prepos-
terous in that its fulfilment is logically impossible; it is also
baneful, because it obscures the actual and very large influence of
concepts upon the process of perception (by which, I must
repeat, I mean something more than the ordinary *reference* of
language to qualities of experience). Every part of the psychology
of perception and attention provides us with examples of how
unverbalized apperceptive reactions are engrained in the content
and structure of the perceptual field. We can also learn from
psychology how perception is affected by verbal cues and
instructions. What remains unstudied is the play of critical
comment in society at large; but we have, each of us in his
own experience, instances of differential emphasis and selective
grouping which have been brought about through the concepts
imparted to us by the writings of critics.

I have perhaps overstressed the role of the critic as teacher,
i.e. as one who affords *new* perceptions and with them new
values. There is such a thing as discovering a community of
perception and feeling which already exists; and this can be a
very pleasant experience. But it often happens that there are
qualities in a work of art which are, so to speak, neither perceived nor ignored but felt or endured in a manner of which
Leibniz has given the classic description. Suppose it is only a
feeling of monotony, a slight oppressiveness, which comes to us
from the style of some writer. A critic then refers to his 'piled-
up clauses, endless sentences, repetitious diction'. This remark
shifts the focus of our attention and brings certain qualities which
had been blurred and marginal into distinct consciousness. When,
with a sense of illumination, we say 'Yes, that's it exactly', we are

really giving expression to the *change* which has taken place in our æsthetic apprehension. The post-critical experience is the true commentary on the pre-critical one. The same thing happens when, after listening to Debussy, we study the chords that can be formed on the basis of the whole-tone scale and then return to Debussy. New feelings are given which bear some resemblance to the old. There is no objection in these cases to our saying that we have been made to 'understand' why we liked (or disliked) the work. But such understanding, which is the legitimate fruit of criticism, is nothing but a second moment of æsthetic experience, a retrial of experienced values. It should not be confused with the psychological study which seeks to know the causes of our feelings.

NOTE

In this article I have tried only to mark out the direction in which, as I believe, the exact nature of criticism should be sought. The task has been largely negative: it is necessary to correct preconceptions, obliterate false trails. There remain questions of two main kinds. Just to establish the adequacy of my analysis, there would have to be a detailed examination of critical phenomena, which present in the gross a fearful complexity. For example, I have paid almost no attention to large-scale or summary judgments—evaluations of artists, schools, or periods. One could quote brief statements about Shakespeare's qualities as a poet or Wagner's as a composer which seem to be full of insight; yet it would be hard to explain what these statements do to our 'perception'—if that word can be used as a synonym for our appreciation of an artist's work as a whole.

But if the analysis is so far correct, it raises a hundred new questions. Two of these—rather, two sides of one large question —are especially important. What is the semantical relationship between the language of criticism and the qualities of the critic's or the reader's experience? I have argued that this relationship is not designation (though I do not deny that there *is* a relationship of designation between the critic's language and *some* qualities of a work of art). But neither is it denotation: the critic does not *point* to the qualities he has in mind. The ostensive function of language will explain the exhibition of *parts* or *details* of an art object but not the exhibition of abstract *qualities*; and it is the latter which is predominant in criticism. The only positive suggestion made in this paper can be restated as follows. To say that the critic 'picks out' a quality in the work of art is to say that if there did exist a designation for that quality, then the designation which the critic employs would be what Morris calls an analytic implicate of that designation. (Thus, 'blue' is an analytic implicate of an expression 'H3B5S2' which designates a certain point on the colour solid.) This definition is clearly not sufficient to characterize the critic's method; but, more, the antecedent of the *definiens* is doubtful in meaning. A study of terms like 'Rembrandt's chiaroscuro', 'the blank verse of *The Tempest*', etc., etc., would probably result in the introduction of an idea analogous to that of the proper name (or of Russell's 'definite description') but with this difference, that the entity uniquely named or labelled by this type of expression is not an object but a quality.

If we put the question on the psychological plane, it reads as follows: How is it that (*a*) we can 'know what we like' in a work of art without (*b*) knowing what 'causes' our enjoyment? I presume that criticism enlightens us as to (*a*) and that (*b*) would be provided by a psychological explanation; also that (*a*) is often true when (*b*) is not.

Contrary to Ducasse[1] and some other writers I cannot see that the critic has any competence as a self-psychologist, a specialist in the explanation of his own responses. There is no other field in which we admit the existence of such scientific insight, unbridled by experimental controls and unsupported by valid general theory; and I do not think we can admit it here. (For that reason I held that critical insight, which does exist, cannot be identified with scientific understanding.) The truth is that, in the present stone age of æsthetic inquiry, we have not even the vaguest idea of the form that a 'law of art appreciation' would take. Consider, 'It is as a *colourist* that Titian excels'; interpret this as a causal hypothesis—for example, 'Titian's colours give pleasure'; and overlook incidental difficulties, such as whether 'colour' means tone or the hue (as opposed to the brightness and the

[1] *Op. cit.*, p. 117.

saturation) of a tone. Superficially, this is similar to many low-grade hypotheses in psychology: 'We owe the *colour* of the object to the retinal rods and cones', 'It is the *brightness* and not the colour that infuriates a bull', 'Highly *saturated* colours give pleasure to American schoolboys'. But the difference is that we do not know what test conditions are marked out by our chosen proposition. Would it be relevant, as a test of its truth, to display the colours of a painting by Titian, in a series of small rectangular areas, to a group of subjects in the laboratory? I cannot believe this to be part of what is meant by a person who affirms this hypothesis. He is committed to no such test.

Anyone with a smattering of Gestalt psychology now interposes that the colours are, of course, pleasing *in* their context, not out of it. One has some trouble in understanding how in that case one could know that it is the *colours* that are pleasing. We may believe in studying the properties of wholes; but it is hard to see what scientific formulation can be given to the idea that a quality should have a certain function (that is, a causal relationship to the responses of an observer) in one and only one whole. Yet that appears to be the case with the colour scheme in any painting by Titian.

We can be relieved of these difficulties simply by admitting our ignorance and confusion; but there is no such escape when we turn to criticism. For it *is* as a colourist that Titian excels—this is a fairly unanimous value judgment, and we should be able to analyse its meaning. (I should not, however, want the issue to turn on this particular example. Simpler and clearer judgments could be cited.) Now when our attention is called, by a critic, to a certain quality, we respond to that quality *in its context*. The context is never specified, as it would have to be in any scientific theory, but always assumed. Every descriptive statement affects our perception of—and our feeling for—the work as a whole. One might say, then, that we agree with the critic if and when he gets us to like the work about as well or as badly as he does. But this is clearly not enough. For he exerts his influence always through a specific discrimination. Art criticism is analytic, discriminating. It concerns itself less with over-all values than with merits and faults in specified respects. It is the quality and not the work that is good or bad; or, if you like, the work is good or bad 'on account of' its qualities. Thus, we may agree with his judgment but reject the critic's grounds (I have shown that the 'grounds' to which he is really appealing are not the same as those which he explicitly states or designates); and when we do this, we are saying that the qualities which he admires are not those which we admire. But then we must know what we admire: we are somehow aware of the special attachment of our feelings to certain abstract qualities rather than to others. Without this, we could never reject a reason given for a value judgment with which we agree—we could never be dissatisfied with descriptive evaluation. There must therefore exist an analysing, sifting, shredding process within perception which corresponds to the conceptual distinctness of our references to 'strong form but weak colour', 'powerful images but slovenly meter', and so on.

This process is mysterious; but we can get useful hints from two quarters. Artists and art teachers are constantly 'experimenting' in their own way. 'Such a bright green at this point is jarring.' 'Shouldn't you add more detail to the large space on the right?' We can compare two wholes in a single respect and mark the difference in the registration upon our feelings. Implicit comparisons of this kind, with shifting tone of feeling, are what are involved in the isolation of qualities from the work, at least in *some* critical judgments. I am afraid that as psychology, as an attempt to discover the causes of our feelings, this is primitive procedure; but as a mere analysis of what is meant by the praise and blame accorded to special qualities, it is not without value.

If, in the second place, we could discover what we mean by the difference between the 'object' and the 'cause' of an emotion, *outside* the field of æsthetics; if we could see both the distinction and the connexion between two such judgments as 'I hate his cheek' and 'It is his cheek that inspires hatred in me'; if we knew what happens when a man says, 'Now I know why I have always disliked him—it is his pretence of humility', there would be a valuable application to the analysis of critical judgments.

CHAPTER IX

THE USE OF 'GOOD' IN ÆSTHETIC JUDGMENTS

By Helen Knight

I

I INTEND to speak about 'good' in such judgments as 'Most of Cézanne's pictures are good', '*Howard's End* is a good novel', 'This is a good film'. But the main points apply to 'beautiful' as much as to 'good'. It is largely a matter of choosing different illustrations for the same general point, and I have chosen 'good' in preference to 'beautiful' as I want to speak about works of art, and, in particular, about pictures. On the whole we commend the works of man for their goodness, and the works of nature for their beauty.

I am raising a philosophic question. When we get into philosophic difficulty about the use of 'good' we are puzzled by the difference between goodness and its criteria, the reasons for goodness—the difference, for example, between 'this is good' and 'this object balances that', 'this line repeats that', 'the placing of this figure brings out the psychological significance of the event'. We become interested in what differentiates the use of 'good' from the use of expressions for its criteria, we become interested in its generality.

This is the problem, and I shall try to show that we can only get light on it by considering the goodness-criteria relation. But this involves a significant denial. Many people have tried to solve their difficulty by giving a naturalistic analysis of 'good' or 'beautiful'. It is suggested, for example, that when anyone says that a work of art is good he means that he likes it, or that it satisfies a desire, or that it gives him a feeling of 'objectified self-affirmation'. But analysis throws no light at all on the goodness-criteria relation, and I shall try to show that no analysis will give us what we want. We shall also see that all naturalistic analyses misrepresent the situation in one way or other.

I will introduce my view by asking you to consider two different uses of 'good', one of which is also a group of uses. There is the use exemplified by 'good tennis player', 'good knitter', 'good Pekingese', 'good piece of steak', etc. We use 'good' in these cases for what is good of its kind. The goodness of these things depends on their satisfying the criteria of goodness for things of their kind. So this use embraces a group of *specific* uses. On the other hand, we have the *general* use exemplified in 'æsthetic experience is good', 'philosophic discussion is good'. We can bring out the contrast by comparing 'philosophic discussion is good' with 'that was a good philosophic discussion', we should use quite different arguments to establish each of these statements.

These uses are different—but in what respects? Certainly not because 'good' occupies different positions in the sentence. It makes no difference to our meaning whether we say 'that tennis player is good' or 'that's a good tennis player'. Whereas we do get the difference when we say 'that discussion was good' (as ordinarily used) and 'discussion is good' (but we might use 'that discussion was good' to exemplify the general use). The difference does not lie in the position of 'good', nor in another and far more important fact. For in *each* case we show the meaning of 'good' by considering its criteria—and not by giving an analysis. There is, however, this difference. Whenever we get a specific 'good' we can always use a certain type of expression—'is a good *picture*', 'is a good *knitter*', 'is a good *Pekingese*' etc.; and the words 'picture', 'knitter', and 'Pekingese' contribute to the meaning of the sentence. But if we try to put the general 'good' in this form we can only get 'is a good *thing*'; and 'is a good thing' means exactly the same as 'is good'. But I want in particular to notice another (though related) difference. It is highly plausible to suppose that my desire for æsthetic experience or philosophic discussion is a criterion for their goodness in the general sense; and, indeed, that my desire for *x* is a criterion for the goodness of *x* in this sense, whatever *x* may be. But it is not plausible to suppose that any of my mental states is a criterion for the goodness of Helen Wills' tennis. The contrast I am pointing to is this: On the one hand we get my desire as a criterion for the goodness of everything that is good in the general sense. On the other hand we get a number of completely different sets of criteria—criteria for tennis, for knitting, for Pekingese dogs, for pieces of steak, and so on. And this is a point I want to emphasize when I class the 'good' of æsthetic judgments among the specific uses.

When we say 'Cézanne's "Green Jar" is good', we are not using 'good' in the general, but in one of the specific senses. It belongs to the group exemplified by 'good tennis playing' and 'good Pekingese'. I shall try to show that this is the natural view to take. And I shall try to say as much as I can about what it involves. The main thing to consider is the goodness-criteria relation. This is the central fact, and explains the generality of 'good'. On the other hand, we must also consider the criteria specific to æsthetic goodness. I propose to discuss the goodness-criteria relation in a relatively simple case, and conclude this discussion with some general observations about the use of 'good'. But all this is extremely difficult, and I know that the discussion is most inadequate; I then hope to show that æsthetic goodness involves this relation. But why, it may be asked, has the point been overlooked? This is not surprising. The æsthetic situation is very complicated, and its complications have obscured the main structure of æsthetic reasoning. But if we see the structure in a simple case we may recognize it in a more complicated one. And accordingly I lay great stress on the analogy.

Suppose I am looking at a game of tennis and say 'that's a good player'. If someone asks me 'why?' or 'what do you mean?' I answer by pointing out features of his playing. I say, for example, that his strokes are swift, that his placing is accurate, and point to the speed of his footwork. In making these remarks I am showing that he satisfies the criteria. I am indicating features of his playing that are criteria for its goodness. And this is what my questioner expected. It is the only answer that any of us expects in our ordinary conversations. We give our meaning by pointing out criterion-characters.

But suppose that my questioner wants a philosophic discussion, and says that this answer neglects the generality of 'good'. It is clear that 'he's a good player' is not equivalent to any one of the reasons suggested above, nor to a group of such reasons. The mere fact of their being *reasons* shows that they are not equivalent, as no proposition is a reason for itself. But it is also obvious that 'he's a good player' says in a sense far less than 'his aim is accurate', and 'she's a good knitter' says far less than 'her knitting is even'. But though 'he's a good player' says less than *one* reason, yet in a sense it stretches over all.

It is at this point that analysis crops up. Suppose we persist in asking 'But what do we mean when we say his playing is good? what are we saying?' We no longer expect the normal answer. We want someone to say: 'I mean by "his playing is good" that it is so-and-so,' where 'so-and-so' is a set of words that provides an analysis. But such an answer, if it could be found, would not really satisfy us. For we want to understand the generality of 'good', and the key to this lies in the goodness-criteria relation. Thus at this point the question: what do we mean? is misleading. For neither an enumeration of criteria nor an analysis will give us what we want.

But let us consider what analysis might be suggested. We shall find the case of knitting quite instructive, for here I can see no candidate at all. It is plain that there just are different criteria, evenness, speed, capacity to do intricate patterns etc. In the case of tennis, someone might suggest 'has winning ability'. It would then be natural to retort: 'and what about style?' This is of course a criterion of goodness, though a steady and reliable player would be good without it. In winning ability and style we have simply found two criteria of a very general type. A player is good *because* of his style and *because* he is able to win. Let us suppose we are looking at two stylish players, neither of whom is able to win. One of them, we can see, is unlikely to improve, in spite of his style he is bad. But the other is promising, 'Look at his style,' we say, 'he is good even though he can't win'. These cases show us something about the goodness-criteria relation. Style is a criterion, but a player may be good without it; and a knitter may be good without speed. On the other hand, a player may have style and not be good, a knitter may be quick and not be good. And consider this: One player is good because of his smashing service and speed of returns, another because of his careful and unexpected placing of the ball, another because of his smashing service and spectacular backhand strokes, another because he never misses a ball. These variations are typical. We sometimes get one set of criteria, sometimes another; and the sets overlap, providing a number of different combinations. It is through considering such examples, and the more of them the better, that we get to know what the goodness-criteria relation is like. It is not, however, just a matter of collecting facts, but of seeing how elastic the relation is.

I shall now attempt to sum up some general points that I think have emerged about the use of 'good', and these contain as much as I can say about its generality. We have seen that the meaning of 'good' is determined by criteria. And this is to say: that the truth and falsity of 'he is a good so-and-so' depends on whether he possesses criterion-characters or not; and that the natural answer to the question, 'what do you mean?' lies in pointing out these characters. But, on the other hand, 'he is a good so-and-so' is not equivalent to any proposition which asserts the possession of a criterion-character, nor to a group of such propositions. This lack of equivalence is marked by the use of 'because' which introduces the criterion propositions. A clear way of stating the difference would be to give a great many cases in which goodness and criterion propositions are differently used. For example: 'he is good, but his placing is not accurate'; 'he is not good, but has a smashing service'; 'he is good, his service is smashing and his returns are speedy'; 'he is good, he is steady and reliable, his service is not smashing and his returns are not speedy'.

On different occasions, as we have seen, we judge by different criteria—'he is good because his service is smashing and his returns are speedy'; 'he is good because he is steady and reliable'. This is certainly not ambiguity. There are not several meanings of 'good' as there are two meanings of 'plain' or two meanings of 'see' when we distinguish 'seeing a physical object' from 'seeing a sense-datum'. The situation, as I have tried to show, is totally different. But none the less I should like to speak about variations in the meaning of 'good', to say that its meaning varies when we use different criteria. Some of the differences, I suggest, are striking enough to merit this description. I shall raise the point later on in connection with æsthetic judgments.

Let us now see how the meaning of 'good' in æsthetic judgments is determined by its criteria. It will be useful to look at a word like 'piquant'. Suppose I say that a certain woman is beautiful, and someone replies 'Not beautiful, but piquant'. I am quite likely to accept this correction, why? Because I see that her features are piquant as distinct from beautiful. And we might point out the marks of piquancy. We might say that her nose is *retroussé*, her chin pointed, her expression vivacious. But in any case we can see that her piquancy depends on her features or expression. And in distinguishing piquancy from beauty we imply that beauty depends on other features (though there may be overlapping).

This example is useful because 'piquant' is the same kind of word as 'good'. But the range of its criteria is narrower, and this makes its dependence on them easier to see. 'Good' is exactly the same kind of word as 'piquant' and 'beautiful', but its use is far wider. It is used with *this* set of criteria and with *that*; and so on through an extremely wide range of overlapping sets. On any *one* occasion it is used with one set only, but on this occasion with this set, on that occasion with that, and so on. This in a way drains it of meaning, it is empty as compared with 'piquant'. So we see the relation between 'piquant' and its criteria more readily, but with a little more attention we can see it just as clearly in the case of 'good'.

Suppose I say that Cézanne's 'Green Jar' is a good picture and someone asks me 'why?' or 'what do you mean?' I should answer by describing it. I should point out a number of facts about its organization, for example: that apple is placed so that it exactly balances the main mass on the right; the lines of table-cloth, knife, and shadows repeat each other; the diagonal of the knife counteracts the diagonals of the shadows. All these objects, I might continue, are exceedingly solid and the shadows exceedingly deep—each thing 'is infallibly in its place'. I might point out a number of important problems that Cézanne has solved; for example, that he combines a geometrical scheme with the variety we get in natural appearances. And finally I might allude to the profundity and gravity of the picture. In this description I have pointed out criterion-characters, the 'Green Jar' is good because it possesses them.

This is the type of reasoning that runs through critical writings. I shall give a few illustrations. Consider Reynolds' discussion of the principal lights in a picture.[1] He praises the 'Bacchus and Ariadne' of Titian. The figure of Ariadne dressed in blue and the sea behind her form a cold contrast to the mellow colours of the principal group. But by giving Ariadne a red scarf and one of the Bacchante some blue drapery Titian prevents a division of the picture into separate sections. On the other hand, Le Brun in 'The Tent of Darius' mismanages the light. The picture has a heavy air because the principal light falls on Statira who is dressed in pale blue. Reynolds then gives the 'Landscape in Moonlight' by Rubens as an example of modifying natural appearance for the sake of harmony. On the one hand Rubens introduces more colour contrast, and on the other hand modifies the natural brightness of the moon. The natural brightness could only be preserved by making everything else very dark. Rembrandt in his 'Man in Armour' preserves the natural brightness of the armour, and as a result the picture is too black. We get a similar type of criterion when Berenson praises Giotto for presenting just those lines, those lights and shadows which convey solidity,[2] and when Fry points out how Cézanne emphasizes just those aspects of colour which convey plastic form.[3] We get quite another type when Reynolds condemns Bernini's 'David' for the meanness of its expression,[4] and Delacroix points out that Millet's peasants are a little too ambitious—this, he explains, is because Millet only reads the Bible.[5]

We find in these cases the same kind of reasoning as in discussions about tennis—he is good because his returns are speedy, it is good because the red scarf and blue drapery preserve the balance. And the question 'what do you mean by saying it's good?' provokes the same kind of answer, 'I mean that the lines balance each other, that it combines geometric structure with variety, that it is profound'.

Let us now consider some cases in which I change my judgment. I decide that a picture is bad. Then someone points out its

[1] *Discourses*, Seeley & Co., London, 1905, pp. 245–52.
[2] *The Italian Painters of the Renaissance*. The Clarendon Press, Oxford, 1930, pp. 70–71.
[3] *Cézanne*. Hogarth Press, London, 1927, pp. 39–40.
[4] *Discourses*, p. 71.
[5] *Journal*, Librairie Plon, Paris, 1893, vol. 2, p. 61.

construction, and I see the picture in a new way. The figures had seemed a mere haphazard collection. I now see a diagonal movement in which the figures participate, and as I follow this movement the space recedes, giving a strong impression of depth. And I reverse my judgment. What determines the change? My perception of how the picture is constructed, my recognition of a criterion-character. Or take these cases. I believe that the 'Death of Chatterton' and the 'Last Goodbye' are good, the one because of its dramatic presentation, the other because of its pathos. But someone convinces me that the one is theatrical and the other sentimental. And I now decide that these pictures are bad.

It is worth while to notice that my *liking* a picture is never a criterion of its goodness. We never say 'this picture is good because I like it'. I fully admit that we value æsthetic experience because it includes enjoyment. It is obvious that liking is important, but we must not mistake its role. It is not a criterion. Nor is it true, as we may be inclined to think, that we always like what we judge to be good, and dislike what we judge to be bad. It is common to find indifference combined with approval— 'I can't see anything in so-and-so, but I believe it's good'. And we also find liking combined with disapproval. I may have a taste for the sentimental, and like *East Lynne*, even if I know that *East Lynne* is sentimental and that sentimentality is bad. Or I may like a novel because it deals with a problem that interests me, and because I agree with its views. But I may believe that its treatment of the problem is unsuited to the novel form. And in both these cases I condemn the novels for the very characters I like.

I have tried to show that the goodness of pictures depends on their possession of criterion-characters. We give reasons for goodness by pointing them out. The judgment 'this is good' or 'this is bad' depends on their presence or absence. And this means that we understand the 'good' of æsthetic judgments by understanding the goodness-criteria relation. Its meaning is determined by criterion-characters, but the proposition 'this is good' is not equivalent to any criterion proposition. And there are rules which determine the truth of the former in relation to the truth of the latter.

And now a few last words about analysis. It is irrelevant to our problem because it tells us nothing about the goodness-criteria relation. I believe we become increasingly convinced of this the more we consider this relation, and that desire for analysis dwindles away. We have indeed found a third alternative, previously overlooked. Our puzzle started when we became convinced that 'good' does not name an indefinable quality, and we tried to remove the puzzle by defining 'good' in naturalistic terms. We now see that 'good' may be indefinable and yet not stand for an indefinable quality, and that it has significance even though in one sense it stands for nothing.

We also see how naturalistic analyses distort the situation. Most of them select a state of mind such as our liking which is not even a criterion of goodness. In looking for such an analysis we tend to look for a mental state which constantly accompanies the judgment that a work of art is good or beautiful. We are struck by some one or other experience such as liking, satisfaction of desire, increased vitality, and analyse æsthetic judgments in terms of this experience. But let us suppose that we *do* find a mental state that constantly accompanies the judgment that a work of art is good or beautiful. What then? It will only provide us with a psychological generalization: whenever anyone judges a work of art to be good he always likes it or it always satisfies a desire, or it always increases his vitality. It does not solve any philosophic problem about the use of 'good'.

2

There are many points to notice about the criteria of æsthetic merit, and many problems to consider. I am passing over many of these, but certainly not because I think them of little importance. I shall first give examples to show the diversity of æsthetic criteria, and then consider variations in the use of 'good' to which this diversity leads. If we look at certain cases of disagreement from this point of view we shall be inclined to interpret them as linguistic differences.

One picture is good for one sort of thing, and another for something quite different. We may praise a water colour for its translucency and an oil for the thickness and richness of its

L

impasto. We praise the brightness and clarity of an Impressionist painting, but do not condemn a Rembrandt for lacking these qualities. It is clear that we look for something different in each case. We praise a Botticelli for the poetry of its theme and a Degas for its realism. And how do we praise a realistic picture? We say that the artist has caught the exact pose, the kind of thing one might see at any moment. And the very banality of that pose (in the case of Degas) is a merit. But we do not condemn Botticelli because we fail to meet his goddesses and nymphs as we walk through the street. On the contrary, we praise him for imagination of the ideal. And we praise him for his flowing rhythm, but do not condemn Byzantine art for being rigid, nor Cézanne for being ponderous. Suppose we are considering the work of a colourist, a member, let us say, of the Venetian school. We praise it for subtle nuances of colour and for atmospheric unity, the kind that obscures the contour of things. We praise it for richness of paint, for richness and vitality of effect. And if it fails in these respects we condemn it. But of course we do not condemn a fresco painting of the fifteenth century because it has none of these qualities. In this kind of painting we look for something quite different, for perfection in each part, for unity achieved by the balance of independent wholes, for simplicity in colour and thinness of paint, for its simple and dignified effect.

These examples show that there are a great many alternative standards. To a large extent these are set by the artist or school. An artist tries to produce a certain effect, and his purpose is shaped by a number of factors: the use of a certain medium (oil, tempera etc.), interest in a certain kind of appearance (sunlight, depth etc.), in a certain kind of form (classical, baroque etc.), in a certain kind of subject (the poetic, the commonplace etc.). All these factors provide criteria, and each provides a large number of alternative criteria. I do not say that the artist's aim is our only critical measure, but it is extremely important and mainly responsible for the diversity of standards.

It is natural to suggest that we can classify criteria, or at least a great many of them, under the headings of form and representation. This classification is convenient and enlightening. But it may suggest misleading ideas. We may think, for example, that we class all formal criteria together because of a common property to which 'formal' refers. But the class of formal properties is heterogeneous. We praise a picture because the parts balance each other, because the colours are orchestrated, because the figures are solid, because the colours are brilliant. These are all formal criteria, but we do not class them together because of a common property. Classification is important, but it does not reduce the diversity of criteria.

I now want to discuss the diversity from the linguistic point of view. We have seen that different pictures are good for different reasons. Accordingly when we say 'this picture is good' we are often judging by different criteria. We can translate this into a statement about language: when we say 'this picture is good' we are often using 'good' with different meanings. Only we must remember that 'good' is not ambiguous, and that the variations of meaning are distinctive.

These variations occur very frequently. We have already seen one reason for this; namely, that pictures are good by different criteria. But there is another reason, that some people *habitually* judge by certain criteria and not by others. It is a commonplace that some people always praise a picture for its form and others for its subject. Each set habitually selects criteria from another group, and, as we shall see, there are other cases. It may be a matter of ignorance. Without historical and technical training we do not know what artists are aiming at, and accordingly are ignorant of a great many criteria. But there is a far more curious reason. We *refuse* to use criteria of which we are well aware. And this is by no means uncommon. Suppose I say to someone that 'After Office Hours' is a good film, and he denies it. I then point out its competent acting, its slickness and smartness. He does not deny that it has these qualities, but answers 'that's not goodness'. But there are many different criteria of goodness in films and these are among them. His answer amounts to saying 'I don't want to accept these criteria of goodness—I don't want to use "good" in this way'. We also get more serious cases of this refusal. Thus Delacroix complains of the 'modern schools' who look on colour as an inferior and 'earthy' aspect of painting, and exhort artists to reject the technique of the colourist. Again what does this come to? 'We don't want to accept these criteria of goodness.' Even Reynolds maintains that the highest art requires simplicity, in fact monotony of colour, and must renounce the harmony of subtle nuances. This partly explains his depreciation of Tintoretto, Veronese and Rubens. And what does his criticism come to? 'I have *decided* to degrade these criteria, and in consequence these artists only paint "ornamental" pictures.'

The point then is this. Either through ignorance or prejudice many people habitually use 'good' with certain meanings and not with others. And when we look at the matter in this light we see that a great deal of æsthetic disagreement is linguistic. It is disagreement in the use of 'good'. Suppose that two people are looking at a picture by Picasso, the kind in which we get abstract treatment of actual objects. One of them says 'this is good' and the other 'this is bad'. The first is judging by its form, and the other points scornfully to the representation (or lack of it). The appropriate comment is, I suggest, 'They are using "good" with different meanings'. And this also applies to the dispute about 'After Office Hours'. But we need not only consider such complete disagreement. Delacroix, for example, places Rubens much higher than Reynolds places him, and this is partly because Delacroix is willing, in fact anxious, to accept colour criteria at their full value.

It is important to notice that when people disagree in this way they may completely agree about the nature of what they are discussing. The filmgoers may agree that 'After Office Hours' is competent in acting, smart and slick. Reynolds fully agrees with Delacroix that Rubens excels in colour technique. This agreement is significant, and fits in very happily with the linguistic explanation. Suppose, on the other hand, that Reynolds was disputing Rubens' excellence as a colourist. This would be a dispute of quite another kind. It would be a factual dispute about Rubens' technique.

There are two more points I must raise before concluding. I shall treat them both in a very sketchy manner, but cannot leave the subject without indicating the lines along which my answer to them would run.

The first is concerned with comparative judgments, 'this picture is better than that'. Such judgments are most profitable when we compare pictures that resemble each other pretty closely, two water colours, two Impressionist paintings, two Baroque paintings, etc. In such cases we judge both pictures by the same criteria.

But what about the comparison of pictures which are good for different reasons? I believe that in some cases this would be nonsensical. It is nonsense to ask whether Raphael or Rembrandt is the better artist, whether rugged scenery is better than soft, or Gothic architecture than Norman. In these cases we can only state a preference for one or the other. But we *do* make comparative judgments where the criteria are different. Raphael's 'School of Athens' is better than a water colour by Crome or a cartoon by Max Beerbohm. But Crome and Beerbohm were aiming at completely different ends from Raphael, and their pictures may be perfect of their kind. The explanation of these comparative judgments is, I believe, that some criteria are higher than others. I mean by this simply that when pictures excel by some criteria we say they are better than if they excel by others. The criteria by which Raphael excels, such as space, composition, organization of groups, expressiveness, dignity, are among the very highest.

The second question is closely connected, and has probably been provoked by many of my statements. What is the guarantee of a criterion? What determines the truth of 'so-and-so is a criterion for goodness in pictures'? The guarantee, I would answer, lies in its being used as a criterion. Organization of groups, space composition, profundity etc., are criteria of goodness because they are used as such. But we must face a difficulty. Who is it that uses them? It is true that some are in general use. A large number of people would praise a picture for its profundity. There is also the important fact that we often use criteria without being able to name or distinguish them. But we must acknowledge that some are only used by critics, and not even by all of them. We must admit that criteria are not firmly fixed, like the points (at any one time) of a Pekingese. But it completely misrepresents the situation to say they are not fixed at all.

Perhaps I should also point out that the fixing of criteria is one thing, and their use another. When we make æsthetic judgments we are using criteria, and not talking about the circumstances in which they are fixed. They are fixed by certain people who no doubt have their reasons for preferring some to others. But we do not refer to these facts in our æsthetic judgments.

I have been constantly harping in this paper on the judicial office of æsthetic judgments, and feel that I must supply an antidote, for I have no desire to exalt this office. I believe, it is true, that the judgments we make in pointing out criteria are the most profitable judgments to make. But we need not make them with judicial intent. It is far better to say 'Cézanne was interested in that and that, we can find so-and-so in his pictures'. The great thing is to discover what a work of art is like.

CHAPTER X

LOGIC AND APPRECIATION

By Stuart Hampshire

IT seems that there *ought* to be a subject called 'Æsthetics'. There is an alexandrianism which assumes that there are so many classified subjects waiting to be discussed and that each one ought to have its place in the library and in the syllabus. There is moral philosophy—the study of the nature of the problems of conduct—in every library and in every syllabus; there ought surely to be a philosophical study of the problems of Art and Beauty—if there are such problems; and this is the question which comes first. That there are problems of conduct cannot be doubted; people sometimes wonder what they ought to do and they find reasons for solving a moral problem to their own satisfaction; one can discuss the nature of these problems, and the form of the arguments used in the solution of them; and this is moral philosophy. But what is the subject-matter of æsthetics? Whose problems and whose methods of solution? Perhaps there is no subject-matter; this would fully explain the poverty and weakness of the books. Many respectable books can be, and have been, written on subjects which have no subject-matter; they may be written for the sake of system and completeness, to round off a philosophy, or simply because it is felt that there ought to be such a subject.

There is a simple and familiar way of finding the subject-matter of æsthetics, by begging the question. One may invent a kind of judgment called a value judgment, and let it be either a judgment about conduct or a judgment about Art and Beauty: a single genus with two species. From this beginning, one may go on to distinguish value judgments from other kinds of judgment. But the existence of the genus has been assumed, the assimilation of moral to æsthetic judgment taken for granted. One has certainly not isolated the subject-matter of æsthetics by this method; the original material has simply been dropped from view. What questions under what conditions are actually answered by æsthetic judgments? This must be the starting-point. I shall argue that æsthetic judgments are not comparable in purpose with moral judgments, and that there are no problems of æsthetics comparable with the problems of ethics.

There are artists who create and invent, and there are critics and a wider audience who appraise and enjoy their work. An artist has the technical problems of the medium in which he works; he may discuss these technical problems with other artists working in the same medium and with those who intimately understand the difficulties of his material. As an artist, he has his own conception of what his own work is to be; clearly or confusedly, he has set his own end before himself; even if his work must satisfy some external demand, he has his own peculiar conception of it, if he is to be regarded as more than a craftsman in some applied art. He has therefore created his own technical problems; they have not been presented to him; they arise out of his own conception of what he is to do. He did not set himself to create Beauty, but some particular thing. The canons of success and failure, of perfection and imperfection, are in this sense internal to the work itself, if it is regarded as an original work of art. In so far as the perfection of the work is assessed by some external criterion, it is not being assessed as a work of art, but rather as a technical achievement in the solution of some presented problem. A work of art is gratuitous. It is not *essentially* the answer to a question or the solution of a presented problem. Anyone may dance for any reason and to achieve any variety of purposes; but a spectator may attend to the movements of the dance for the sake of their own intrinsic qualities, and disregard the purposes which lie outside; and, so regarded, the dance becomes gratuitous; it ceases to be an action, and becomes a set of movements; the subject of the spectator's attention has changed.

Compare the subject-matter and situation of moral judgment. Throughout any day of one's life, and from the moment of waking, one is confronted with situations which demand action. Even to omit to do anything positive, and to remain passive, is to adopt a policy; Oblomov had his own solution to the practical problems confronting him; his was one possible solution among others. One can suspend judgment on theoretical questions and refuse either to affirm or to deny any particular solution; but no one can refuse to take one path or another in any situation which confronts him; there must always be an answer to the question 'What did you do in that situation?' even if the answer is: 'I ignored it and did nothing; I went to bed and to sleep'. If that is the answer, that was the solution adopted. One can always describe, first, the situation and the possibilities open, and, secondly, the solution of the problem which the agent adopted. Action in response to any moral problem is not gratuitous; it is imposed; that there should be some response is absolutely necessary. One cannot pass by a situation; one must pass *through* it in one way or another.

When there are unavoidable problems, a rational man looks for some general method of solving them; a rational man may be defined as a man who adheres to general methods, allotting to each type of problem its own method of solution. Unless general methods of solution are recognized, there can be no grounds for distinguishing a valid from an invalid step in any argument in support of any solution. To be irrational is either to have no reasons at all for preferring one solution to another, or to give utterly different reasons in different cases of the same type; to refuse any general method of solving problems of a particular type is to accept either caprice or inconsistency in that domain. 'Must there be some general method of solving problems of conduct?' Or 'Must to act rightly be to act rationally and consistently?'—these have always been the principal questions in moral philosophy. Aristotle, the most accurate of moral philosophers, gave a carefully ambiguous answer, Kant an unambiguous 'Yes', Hume a qualified 'No'; for Hume held that morality was ultimately a matter of the heart and not of the head, of sympathy and not of consistency. But none of these philosophers denied that it always makes sense to ask for the reasons behind any practical decision; for constant ends may be served by a variety of different means. Actions (unlike works of art) do not bear their justification on the face of them; one must first inquire into reasons and purposes. Even if it is not necessary, at least it is always possible, to adopt some general ends of action, or (it is ultimately the same) to acknowledge some universal principles. Since any action susceptible of moral judgment can be viewed as the solution of a problem presented, one can always criticize and compare different methods of solution. Consistent policies are needed in order to meet common human predicaments; men may discuss the reasons which have inclined them to solve the same problem in different ways. Their arguments (since arguments must be consistent) will lead them to general principles; anyone, therefore, who moralizes necessarily generalizes; he 'draws a moral'; in giving his grounds of choice, he subsumes particular cases under a general rule. Only an æsthete in action would comfortably refuse to give any grounds of decision; he might refer the questioner to the particular qualities of the particular performance; precisely this refusal to generalize would be the mark of his æstheticism. Virtue and good conduct are essentially repeatable and imitable, in a sense in which a work of art is not. To copy a right action is to act rightly; but a copy of a work of art is not necessarily or generally a work of art.

In a moralizing climate there will always be a demand, based on analogy, for principles of criticism, parallel with principles of conduct. But this analogy must be false. Where it makes sense to speak of a problem, it makes sense to speak of a solution of it; and where solutions are offered, it makes sense to ask for reasons for preferring one solution to another; it is possible to demand consistency of choice and general principles of preference. But if something is made or done gratuitously, and not in response to a problem posed, there can be no question of preferring one solution to another; judgment of the work done does not involve a choice, and there is no need to find grounds of preference. One may, as a spectator, prefer one work to another, but there is no *necessity* to decide between them; if the works themselves are regarded as free creations, to be enjoyed or neglected for what they are, then any grading is inessential to the judgment of them; if they are not answers to a common problem, they do not compete and neither need be rejected, except on its own merits. A critical judgment is in this sense non-committal and makes no recommendation; the critic may reject the work done without being required to show what the artist ought to have done in place of the work rejected. But the moralist who

condemns an action must indicate what ought to have been
done in its place; for something had to be done, some choice
between relative evils made. All practical decision is choice
between relative evils or relative goods; if what was done was
wrong, the agent must have failed to do what he ought to have
done. Any moral comment has therefore some force of recommendation and is itself a practical judgment. A moral censor
must put himself in the place of the agent and imaginatively
confront the situation which the agent confronted; the censor
and the agent censored have so far the same problem. But a
critic is not another artist, as the moral censor is another agent;
he is a mere spectator and he has the spectator's total irrespon-
sibility; it is only required that he should see the object exactly
as it is. Nothing which he says in judgment and description
necessarily carries any exclusions with it, or necessarily reflects
upon the merit of other work; the possible varieties of beautiful
and excellent things are inexhaustible. He may therefore discuss
any work on its merits alone, in the most strict sense of this
phrase; he need not look elsewhere and to possible alternatives
in making his judgment. On the contrary, his purpose is to
lead people *not* to look elsewhere, but to look here, at precisely
this unique object; not to see the object as one of a kind, but to
see it as individual and unrepeatable.

One engages in moral argument in order to arrive at a
conclusion—what is to be done or ought to have been done;
one had the practical problem to begin with, and the conclusion
('this is better than that') is always more important than the
route by which one arrives at it; for one *must* decide one way or
the other. But a picture or poem is not created as a challenge or
puzzle, requiring the spectator to decide for or against. One
engages in æsthetic discussion for the sake of what one might
see on the way, and not for the sake of arriving at a conclusion,
a final verdict for or against; if one has been brought to see what
there is to be seen in the object, the purpose of discussion is
achieved. Where the logicians' framework of problem and
conclusion does not apply, the notion of 'reason' loses some of its
meaning also; it is unnatural to ask '*why* is that picture or sonata
good?' in parallel with 'why was that the right thing to do?'
There are no reasons why some object is ugly in the sense that

there are reasons why some action is wrong. Perhaps it may be said that there are particular features of the particular object which *make* it ugly or beautiful, and these can be pointed out, isolated, and placed in a frame of attention; and it is the greatest service of the critic to direct attention in this analytical way. But when attention is directed to the particular features of the particular object, the point is to bring people to see these features, and not simply to lead them to say: 'That's good'. There is no point in arguing that the object is good *because* it possesses these qualities, if this involves the generalization that all objects similar in this respect are good; for if one generalizes in this manner, one looks away from the particular qualities of the particular thing, and is left with some general formula or recipe, useless alike to artist and spectator. One does not need a formula or recipe unless one needs repetitions; and one needs repetitions and rules in conduct, but not in art; the artist does not need a formula of reproduction and the spectator does not need a formula of evaluation.

The spectator-critic in any of the arts needs gifts precisely the opposite of the moralist's; he needs to suspend his natural sense of purpose and significance. To hold attention still upon any particular thing is unnatural; normally, we take objects—whether perceived by sight, touch, hearing, or by any combination of the senses—as signs of possible actions and as instances of some usable kind; we look through them to their possible uses, and classify them by their uses rather than by sensuous similarities. The common vocabulary, being created for practical purposes, obstructs any disinterested perception of things; things are (in a sense) recognized before they are really seen or heard. There is no practical reason why attention should be arrested upon a single object, framed and set apart; attention might always be practical attention, and therefore always passing from one thing to the next; in the sense in which thunder 'means' rain, almost everything means something else; 'what does it mean?' is the primitive reaction which prevents perception. One may always look through a picture as if it were a map, and look through a landscape towards a destination; for everything presented through the senses arouses expectations and is taken as a signal of some likely reaction. Nothing but holding an object still in attention, by itself and for its own sake, would count as having an æsthetic interest in it. A great part of a critic's work, in any of the arts, is to place a frame upon the object and upon its parts and features, and to do this by an unnatural use of words in description. Perception, of any kind and on any level, has degrees; some perceive more than others, and it is difficult to see and hear all that there is to see and hear. There is a metaphysical prejudice that the world consists of so many definite objects possessing so many definite qualities, and that, if we perceive and attend to the objects, we necessarily notice their qualities; as if the things and their qualities were somehow already isolated and labelled for us, ready for the camera-brain to record. So it seems that in principle a vast inventory might be made of all the things in the world with their qualities, passively received and recorded; when one had gone through the inventory of literal description, any further statements about the furniture of the world would be subjective impression and metaphor. There is the prejudice that things really do have colours and shapes, but that there do not exist, literally and objectively, concordances of colours and perceived rhythms and balances of shapes; these are supposed to be added by the mind. It seems that the more recondite qualities of form, expression, style, atmosphere, cannot properly be entered in the inventory of the world, alongside the weights and measures of things; the relations of stress and balance between masses in sculpture or building cannot *really* be seen in any literal sense; the expression of a voice is not as much a perceptible reality as its loudness. The qualities which are of no direct practical interest are normally described metaphorically, by some transference of terms from the common vocabulary; and the common vocabularly is a vocabulary of action, classifying by use and function. The assumption is that only these literal descriptions are descriptions of realities; so descriptions of æsthetic qualities become subjective impressions. But a colony of æsthetes, disengaged from practical needs and manipulations, would single out different units of attention (things), and they would see different resemblances and make different comparisons (qualities). Descriptions of æsthetic qualities, which for us are metaphorical, might seem to them to have an altogether literal and familiar sense. They might find complete agreement among themselves in the use of a more directly descriptive vocabulary, singling out different units of attention. A critic in any one of the arts is under the necessity of building such a vocabulary in opposition to the main tendency of his language; he needs somehow to convince himself that certain isolated objects of his attention really do have the extraordinary qualities which they seem to have; to this end he will need to discuss his perceptions with others, and to try to bring others to notice these qualities. He may have seen (in the wider sense of 'see') more than there is to be seen; and the only test of whether the qualities are really there must be some agreement among careful and disinterested observers. This is the point at which an æsthetic judgment is made—what are the relationships of elements here? What pattern or arrangement of elements is there to be seen, when one attends to the thing carefully and disinterestedly? Anything may be seen or heard or read in many different ways, and as an arrangement of any number of elements of different kinds. The picking out of the elements and of their pattern, in defiance of habit and practical interest, is a work of practice and skill; and the use of words in description is an aid to this perception. Anything whatever may be picked out as an object of æsthetic interest—anything which, when attended to carefully and apart altogether from its uses, provides, by the arrangement of its elements and their suggestion to the imagination, some peculiar satisfaction of its own. An æsthetic judgment has to point to the arrangement of elements, and to show what constitutes the originality of the arrangement in this particular case; what one calls originality in one case may bear little analogy to originality found elsewhere; for there was no common problem to be solved and the achievements were essentially different.

But a moralist in criticism (and there exist such critics) will always be making unnecessary choices and laying down principles of exclusion, as a moralist must. He will make 'value judgments', and a value judgment is essentially a grading of one thing as better than another. If the judgment is an assessment of the particular excellences of works which are very similar, it may be enlightening and useful; but there can be larger comparisons of scale and greatness between things which are in themselves very different. Judgments of this second kind may be taken as practical advice that certain things ought to be read, seen, and heard, and the advice must involve some reference to the whole economy of human needs and purposes; but at this point the critic has actually become a moralist, and the arguments supporting his recommendations are the subject-matter of ethics. 'Is this thing more worth attention than other objects of its kind?' is one question, and 'What is the peculiar arrangement of elements here and what are the effects of this arrangement?' is another. Most æsthetic theories have involved a confusion of answers to these two very different questions; no positive answer to the second by itself entails any answer to the first. One would need to add some further premises about changing human needs and interests; and there is no reason to assume that all works of art satisfy the same needs and interests at all times and for all people. The objects themselves, and the artists who made them, make no unavoidable claim on the spectator's interest, and anyone may neglect the work done when it is of no interest to him. But the peculiar features of particular objects, with their own originality of arrangement, remain constant and unaffected by the spectator's choices and priorities; and there can be no place for exclusive theories and general principles in identifying their originality; they must be seen as they are, individually, and not judged as contestants in a single race called Art or The Novel or Painting.

I conclude that everyone needs a morality to make exclusions in conduct; but neither an artist nor a critical spectator unavoidably needs an æsthetic; and when in Æsthetics one moves from the particular to the general, one is travelling in the wrong direction.

CHAPTER XI

ART AND THE 'OBJECT OF ART'

By Paul Ziff

PERHAPS the most persistent myth in present-day æsthetics is the notion that when we discuss a work of art we are not talking about a painting but about some 'illusory' or 'imaginary' thing sometimes called the 'object of art' or the 'æsthetic object'. I can best explain what this myth is by quoting a statement of Samuel Alexander.

> More than once I have pointed out how in the beautiful object the significance is supplied in part from the artist's mind; how it is he who makes the flat Madonna seem, as Mr. Berenson puts it, a tangible three-dimensional being, or who gives divine playfulness to the Hermes, or motion and dance to the motionless maidens in the picture of the Spring, or who finds the perfect, the only fitting word, to express a meaning that springs from him, . . . And I have contrasted the object of art with the mere percept where also half comes from the perceiver's mind and half from what he directly sees: the coloured moving shape is perceived to be a man, though sight alone without memory does not say so. The contrast . . . is this: the characters we impute to the object perceived, if we perceive correctly, really do belong to the object and may be sensed there on proper occasion; the coloured shape is the visible surface of a man; but in the work of art there is always illusion: the Hermes is not divine only but seems so, and the girls in the Spring are not in motion. At the same time, I have added, the artistic illusion is unlike ordinary perceptual illusion, for that illusion disappears to better acquaintance, is recognized to be an illusion. Whereas the illusion is of the essence of the work of art—ceases, therefore, to be illusion and makes the object significant.
>
> *Philosophical and Literary Pieces*, p. 259.

Let me state the kind of thing Alexander is talking about; for even though he expresses himself with admirable clarity, it is always useful to state a point in as simple a manner as is possible. And let us take some particular example; say, a Cézanne still-life of some apples. When we describe Cézanne's painting we may say 'the apples are solid, round full-volumes—like tangible three-dimensional things. The painting has great depth.' But a painting is a thin strip of canvas covered with tiny pellets of pigment. The canvas is flat, but the work of art has great depth? Thus Alexander arrives at the view that the work of art is distinct from the painting; for the characters we impute to the painting do not really belong to it. We speak of solid voluminous apples, but there are only thin pellets of pigment on the surface of the canvas. Thus there is an illusion, and this illusion is the object of art, that which we call beautiful, that which we judge, criticize, evaluate, and, in general, discuss. It is as simple as this.

Before examining this argument we should notice that Alexander is not alone among æstheticians in adopting such a view. For analogous reasons Collingwood has claimed that the work of art is an 'imaginary object'. And, in a similar vein, S. C. Pepper contends that the work of art is our 'perceptions' of the painting. De Witt Parker, following Bosanquet, held quite similar views. Of course, not all these æstheticians agree that there is an illusion involved in our perception of a painting, but they all maintain, along with Alexander, that there is a significant discrepancy between the painting and the work of art. That is to say, they agree with Alexander in claiming that the characters we impute to the painting do not really belong to the painting, but rather, are characters of the work of art. Just what the work of art is held to be, varies from one philosopher to another; for Collingwood it is an 'imaginary object'; Pepper contends that it is a 'series of intermittent perceptions'; Alexander insists it is an 'illusion'; and so forth. But all agree that the painting is not the work of art. Indeed, it would not be too far amiss to say that the prevalent opinion in æsthetics is in general accordance with Alexander's account. And this is why it is important to show and to show clearly, how very mistaken this view is.

I

First of all we must consider the notion that there is an illusion involved in observing a painting. This particular point is, as we have already mentioned, somewhat peculiar to Alexander. For although other æstheticians claim there is a discrepancy between the characters we impute to the painting and the characters it actually possesses, few are prepared to maintain that there is any illusion at work here. Thus, even though we may succeed in dispelling the illusion that there is illusion involved in observing

M

a painting, we shall not have dispelled the more significant and more momentous illusion that there is some discrepancy between the characters we impute to the painting and the characters the painting actually possesses. Nonetheless, it is fruitful to begin our discussion by pointing out that all talk of illusion is wholly mistaken. For although it does not follow from the fact that there is no illusion at work here, that the characters we impute to the painting really do belong to the painting, it would follow from the fact—if it were a fact—that there is an illusion at work here that the characters we impute to the painting do not really belong to the painting. Thus it is quite important to show that there is no illusion at work here, even though showing this does not prove all that we want to prove. To show that all talk of illusion is quite mistaken we must take pains to make clear just what is meant in speaking of an illusion.

A traveller crossing a desert may suddenly see a clear lake spread out before him. He stares at it in amazement, rubs his eyes and looks again. The waters beckon him; he rushes forward and plunges his hand into hot sand. He was the victim of a mirage—an illusion. He thought there was water there, it looked like water, but in fact it was only sand. This is one example of what an illusion is like. Suppose someone suffers from hallucinations, and further suppose he sees an illusory apple on a table before him. He thinks an apple is there, he sees an apple, but when he reaches out to grasp it, there is nothing to be grasped. He is deceived, for he too is the victim of an illusion. Mirages and hallucinations are but two types of visual illusions. There are others still more common. But there are other things which are sometimes loosely spoken of as 'illusions' which are usually not illusions at all. For example, if we asked someone to describe what he sees when he looks at railroad tracks he might say 'They look as if they converge in the distance'. We are all familiar with this sort of description of railroad tracks. And if anyone said this we shouldn't feel anything wrong with what he was saying. For, in a way, they do look as if they converge, even though we all know that they do not. You can look long and hard at railroad tracks, squint your eyes and peer off into the distance, but they still look as if they converge, even though they do not in fact converge. But, ordinarily, there is nothing illusory about looking at railroad tracks, for no one is deceived. If a child, say, were to look at the railroad tracks and ask 'how do the trains run on the tracks when they come together?' in such a case we would feel inclined to speak of an illusion. This point can, perhaps, be made clear by considering the matter in a slightly different fashion. Suppose a prankster laid out some railroad tracks which, instead of running parallel to one another, diverged in such a manner as to make them look parallel. Would anyone who stood at the right point on the tracks and looked off into the distance say 'The tracks look as if they run parallel'? Someone could describe what he saw in that way, but, most likely, he would be too amazed to say anything at all. Indeed, he would think he was suffering from an illusion. But suppose he said to someone who was not looking at these queer tracks 'The tracks look as if they run parallel to one another'. The person who heard this would, most likely, not be the least astonished. For example, a railroad foreman could ask one of his crew to take a look at the tracks they had just laid to see if they were parallel. He might be told that 'The tracks look as if they run parallel', and such a response would not be apt to make him stare in amazement. The point is that we can and do describe what we see when we look at ordinary railroad tracks by saying either 'The tracks look as if they run parallel' or 'The tracks look as if they converge'. We should not ordinarily say that either description is the report of an illusion. For whether or no we say a particular description is the report of an illusion depends on whether the person who gives the description of what he sees is likely to be deceived or not.

Let us now consider what happens when we observe a painting, and whether there is anything in such a situation which can properly be spoken of as an illusion. Suppose, while looking at a Cézanne still-life, we say 'It has great depth. The apples pictured are full, solid volumes.' This is the kind of statement we make when, say, we are in a painting gallery and are discussing the painting. In saying this I do not wish to suggest that we are apt to make this statement only in such a situation, for this is not true. There are many situations, many different ones, in which we make exactly the same statement. All I wish to suggest is that at least one of the situations where we make such a statement is the one I have just mentioned. When we are in the painting gallery discussing the painting, and when we say 'The painting has great depth', are we deceived into believing that we could walk through the canvas, put our hands in it, move around inside? Does the canvas look as though we could walk into and through it? The canvas looks as though it has great depth? Another way of putting this question is to ask: does the frame around the painting look, say, like the frame of an open window? Or like a doorway through which we could pass freely? We often do say that a painting is very much like a window; a window through which we can see all kinds of strange and fascinating things which cannot be seen through any ordinary window. But when we see an ordinary open window it really does look as though we can pass through the window. But when we see a painting which we sometimes speak of as a window through which to view the world, it does not really look as though we could pass our hands and feet through it. Not at all. The canvas looks flat just as it is flat. Are we to suppose when Alexander first saw the 'flat Madonna' he speaks of, that he couldn't see that the picture of the Madonna was painted on a flat canvas?—that the painted canvas didn't look flat to him? Did he have to go up and look closely at the canvas to see that it actually was flat, and that it would be quite futile for him to attempt to clamber through? This seems most unlikely. For the only type of painting where the canvas doesn't look flat is what we call a work of *trompe l'œil*—and the name is tailor-made; for it is a type of painting where the artist has amused himself, and possibly his audience, by creating optical illusions. When we first look at this sort of work we are deceived and fail to realize that we are looking at a painting. In observing a work of *trompe l'œil* we are apt to suppose that the picture of an apple is not a picture but a real apple. The apple looks as though we could take it in our hands. And people sometimes are deceived. Just as children might be deceived by the illusion of railroad tracks converging and might have to be taken for a walk along the tracks to be convinced that they do not in fact converge, so people sometimes must touch the canvas, must peer at it, to convince themselves that the picture of an apple is indeed just that, not a real apple after all. But neither Cézanne's paintings nor the Renaissance Madonnas are works of *trompe l'œil*. If Alexander was correct in claiming that 'the illusion is of the essence of the work of art' and if this kind of illusion is the kind he is talking about then there would be no way of distinguishing a work of *trompe l'œil* from any other work—but in fact we do make such a distinction. (It is true that it is hard to draw a clear-cut line between those works which are properly spoken of as works of *trompe l'œil* and those which are not. For here, as everywhere, there are borderline cases. Thus red merges imperceptibly into blue—but who would on that account say that red is blue?) It is true that there are paintings which produce optical illusions, and the fact that they do is adequately indicated by the way we label them. For in calling them works of *trompe l'œil* we wish to signalize that these paintings do deceive the eye, and in this respect are quite unlike other paintings which are not works of *trompe l'œil*. Thus it is quite true to say that there are some paintings which produce optical illusions, and if this was what Alexander was saying then he would be perfectly correct. However, it is completely obvious that this is not what Alexander was saying. For I take it that when he says 'the illusion is of the essence of the work of art', he is saying that every work of art has something to do with an illusion and not merely that there are some works of art which have something to do with an illusion. Thus unless we are prepared to maintain the false view that all paintings are works of *trompe l'œil* and not merely that some are, we have, as yet, seen no evidence which would warrant Alexander's statement that 'the illusion is of the essence of the work of art'. And we must note that even though there are some paintings which have something to do with an illusion, these paintings are relatively few in number, indeed, quite scarce, and they are of slight interest to the æsthetician. By far the greatest number of paintings are, in this respect, like Cézanne's canvases. The canvases are flat and they appear flat, they are seen as flat, they look flat. No one is ever deceived.

We have seen that one important characteristic of illusions is not applicable to paintings. This is the fact that we are deceived by illusions, but we are not deceived by any ordinary painting. This is, in itself, sufficient to indicate that all talk of illusion is quite misleading. But we need not stop here, for, as we press the matter, it becomes more and more apparent that there can be no question of an illusion. A person on the desert might be familiar with mirages and thus might not be deceived by what he sees. Thus, in this case, looking at the painting might be analogous to looking at the mirage, for in neither case is there any deception. But the similarity between the two cases begins and ends at this point. No one has to study the mirage, examine and grow familiar with it before he says 'It looks as if there is a lake in the distance'. For a single glance will suffice to reveal the lake in the distance. But this is totally unlike what occurs when people look at a Cézanne painting. It may take some time to see the depth in one of his paintings; the observer must first grow familiar with the painting, get to know it by carefully examining the structure, composition, design, and so forth. Of course, there are many paintings which do not require such extensive study. For example, even a quick look at Rembrandt's 'Night Watch' will suffice to show that it is a picture of a group of figures, some in front of others. But there are many paintings for which a brief glance will not suffice to disclose the volumes and spaces and, with such a painting, we must first get to know it quite well before we can see its depth. An analogy with music may be useful here. This process of getting to know a painting has its counterpart in the process of getting to know a piece of music. When we first hear a somewhat complex work, say a Bach violin partita, we may have difficulty in recognizing the themes and in following the variations. When we do know the work we can then hear the themes clearly. Can we say that this process of getting to know a work of art is the progressive growth of an illusion? If to see the volumes and space in a painting is to have an illusion then it seems we should describe this process of getting to know a painting as the progressive growth of an illusion, the deliberate cultivation of an hallucination. But if this is an illusion it certainly is unlike anything else which we ordinarily call an illusion. Indeed, it is so unlike anything which is ordinarily called an illusion that it seems quite grotesque to speak of it in this way. Finally, after having managed to see the depth in a Cézanne painting, we can often revert to our original way of seeing it. That is, sometimes we can choose to see it as having depth or to see it as flat. But who can do this with an illusion?

For the illusion of the lake in the distance is not something that can be dispelled at will. And the same thing is true of all illusions. But this is totally unlike the so-called 'illusion' of space in the Cézanne still-life. For in looking at a Cézanne still-life we can often choose either to see the painting as flat or to see it as having depth.

So far we have failed to produce any evidence for Alexander's statement 'the illusion is of the essence of the work of art'. But we cannot leave the matter like this. For, from what has so far been said, it would seem that Alexander was an utterly confused thinker and had not the slightest idea of what an illusion was like. And this, of course, is absolutely false. I do think Alexander is mistaken in what he says, but I do not think it is a foolish or a naïve mistake. And if we cannot present what he is saying in a more plausible light, this only points to a failure in our analysis. However, I think we can make his position seem quite plausible if we approach it in a certain manner. It was mentioned above that we often do say a painting is very much like a window. And we argued that looking at a painting is, except perhaps with works of *trompe l'œil*, not at all like looking at an open window. And I still believe that what we said is quite true. But we failed to point out that looking at a painting may seem very much like looking at a closed window, and it may also seem very much like looking through a closed window. For example, someone standing before a closed window may look through the glass at, say, the landscape outside. But he may also look at the glass of the window. Similarly, someone standing before a painting may look, as it were, through the canvas and see a new and fascinating landscape. But he may also look at the canvas. Now when we look at a closed window, especially if the glass is somewhat dusty, we do not think we can pass through the window, for we know quite well that the glass will prevent us from doing this. It does not look as though we could actually pass through the glass, and the only time it would look that way is when the window looks just like an open window. Nonetheless, we can look through the glass, and we know that what we see is on the other side of the glass. Thus looking at a painting seems very much like looking at a somewhat dusty window. But when we look through the canvas we know that what we see is not on the

other side of the canvas. For what we see when we look through
the canvas is no-where and no-when. The canvas looks as though
there is something beyond it, but in fact there is nothing. Thus
there is an illusion. When we look through a window we look
at, say, the landscape. But when we look through the canvas we
look at the æsthetic object, the work of art. Thus the work of
art is akin to the Red Queen in that it too exists only on the other
side of the glass. And this is a very persuasive picture of what
does transpire when we look at paintings.

But even though this account is persuasive when looked at
in one way, if we approach it with a critical eye its persuasiveness
can be dispelled. For, in fact, looking through a canvas is quite
unlike looking through a glass, and this despite the fact that an
analogy can be made out between them. When we look through
a glass—even a dusty one—it does look as though we could walk
around in the space beyond the glass, as though there is a place
for head and hands and feet on the other side of the glass. But
when we look through a canvas it does not look at all like this.
The only time it would look like this is when we look at works
of *trompe l'œil*. And we have already pointed out that these are
very special and rare cases. If when we looked through what we
took to be a window, even a dusty window, we found that there
was nothing outside, no other side to the glass, we should be
astounded. For, in such a case, we assume that it did look as
though there was something on the other side of the glass. It
would be like looking across the room through a dusty window
at what we took to be the house across the street only to find
that some astounding artist had painted the whole scene on our
window pane. In such a case it really would look as though
there was something on the other side of the glass. I submit
that this is not at all like what does happen when we look at an
ordinary painting, or even when we look through an ordinary
painting. And it is no good saying that if we put the painting
in the window frame in place of the glass and if we arranged the
lighting in a certain way and if we then had a person look at it
who didn't know what had been done, then it would look to
him as though there was something on the other side of the
painting. For all this is to say no more than that if the painting
didn't look the way it does in fact ordinarily look, then it might

look as though there was something on the other side of the painting. And for all I know perhaps we could play such tricks with paintings, but whether it could be done or not is totally irrelevant to what I am saying. For in saying that when we look through a painting it does not look as though there is something on the other side of the painting, I am not talking about what might be the case. I am talking only about what is the case, and the fact that something else might be the case doesn't in the least matter.

Thus, we may repeat, we have not as yet found any evidence which would warrant Alexander's statement that 'the illusion is of the essence of the work of art'. Perhaps this is due to the fact that, as Alexander states, 'the artistic illusion is unlike ordinary perceptual illusion'. And we must admit that it is unlike ordinary perceptual illusion, very much unlike it. Indeed, so very much unlike anything we ordinarily speak of as an illusion that, as yet, we haven't seen the slightest reason for speaking of it as an illusion. However, we need not labour this point. It is clear that Alexander did think something dreadfully queer was going on and he used the word 'illusion' to describe it. And one of the things that he, along with some other æstheticians, finds dreadfully queer is the way we ordinarily talk about paintings. Here we have the real question.

2

The real question before us is, to use Alexander's terms, whether the characters we impute to a painting really do belong to the painting or not. Alexander, along with some other æstheticians, claims that they do not. Thus they claim that we often say things about paintings which are not in fact true of the paintings. Of course, they do not claim that none of the things we say about paintings are in fact true of the paintings, but only that some of the things we say about paintings are not in fact true. And what is more, it is the important and interesting things we say about paintings that are not in fact true. For example, such statements as 'The painting has great depth', 'The apples pictured are full of solid volumes', etc., are held to be not in fact true. Now it is not too difficult to see one reason why they are inclined to say this. There are times when we point

to a painting by Cézanne and say 'It has great depth'. And there
are times when we point to the same painting and say 'It is flat'.
Alexander, having caught hold of these two, quite different,
descriptions is troubled how to put them together. The painting
can't both have great depth and be flat—this sounds like a
contradiction. Hence, he reasons, when we say the painting has
depth we are suffering from an illusion.

Now I want to say that a Cézanne painting really does have
great depth. We are not victimized by an illusion, nor are we
suffering from an hallucination, when we say of the apples in a
Cézanne still-life, that one apple is in front of the other. Nor
are we speaking of what seems to be the case instead of what
actually is the case. One apple is in front of the other, the painting
does have great depth. Thus there is nothing to be explained
away. But there is a confusion which must be eliminated. Let
there be no mistake about what is being said here. Alexander
says that the Madonna is flat, the Hermes is not divine but only
seems so, the girls in the Spring are not in motion—they too
only seem so. Now I cannot say whether the Hermes Alexander
speaks of is divine or not, for I do not know which statue he is
referring to. But if, when he speaks of the girls in the Spring,
he is referring to Botticelli's 'Primavera', then, of course, the girls
are in motion. There is no question of it merely seeming to be
the case, it is the case. Furthermore, let it be clear that it is the
painting I am talking about, not some 'illusory object' or
'imaginary object' or a 'series of intermittent perceptions'.

There are many ways of describing a painting. We can say
'The painting is flat' and we can also say 'The painting has great
depth'. We can say 'It is a painting of apples, all of which are
about the same size, with some close up and others off in the
distance'. We can also say 'It is a painting of apples, all of which
are different sizes, some large and placed towards the bottom of
the canvas, and others small at the top of the canvas'. (We can
also describe what we see and speak of how the painting looks,
but the use of this sort of description is not germane to our
problem.) Difficulties arise only if we suppose that all of these
descriptions have the same use, only if we confuse the use of
these various descriptions.

We can imagine a curious sort of game that might be played

here to clarify our problem. Suppose we set ourselves the task
of describing a Cézanne painting, and we wished to describe it
in all sorts of ways. First, we might say the painting is a flat
pigment-coated strip of canvas mounted on wooden stretchers.
If we were to go to a carpenter and ask him to build a crate for
shipping the painting we might say to him 'The crate needn't
be very wide; it will be used to ship an ordinary painting'. It
would be important in this case for the carpenter to realize that
the painting we wish to ship is made of a flat strip of canvas
mounted on wooden stretchers, for some paintings are executed
on gesso panels, some on masonite, and some on plaster slabs,
and so forth. The width of the crate required might vary in
different cases. Secondly, we might say that painting is a strip
of linen canvas coated with pigments containing manganese
oxides, iron hydroxides, and so forth. This would be important
and relevant to a chemist engaged in cleaning the painting. It
might also be of interest to someone planning to purchase the
painting for he would probably wish to know whether the
colours are especially apt to fade. Thirdly, we might say it is a
painting of apples, all of which are different sizes, some large
and placed towards the bottom of the canvas, and others small
towards the top. This would be like describing a picture of two
people, one close up and the other off in the distance, as a picture
of one very big person and another very tiny person. Even this
queer sort of description occasionally has a use. For example, it
would be relevant to describe the picture as consisting of large and
small apples to an art student intent on copying the painting. For
example, we might say to him 'You have drawn the apple towards
the top of the canvas much too large. The one in the painting you
are supposed to be copying is a very small apple.' Fourthly, we
might say it is a painting of apples, all of which are about the
same size, with some close up and others off in the distance.
This is, perhaps, the most familiar kind of description of a
painting. When we ask 'What is the painting of?' this is one sort
of answer that might be relevant. In short, it is what we usually
call a description of the subject-matter of the painting. Fifthly,
we might say it is a painting with strong two-dimensional
movements contrasted with a diagonal three-dimensional movement. Or we might say simply, the painting has great depth. This

is the sort of description a person who criticizes, judges, evaluates, or simply appreciates, the painting would be primarily interested in. There are, of course, still many other kinds of descriptions that might be given, but these are sufficient for our purposes.

Lest there be any misunderstanding of what has been said, let me say explicitly that in providing examples of how these various descriptions are sometimes used I do not, by any means, wish to suggest that they are used only in the ways mentioned. For this is plainly untrue. Nor do I wish to suggest that the examples given are to be taken as typical instances of how these various descriptions are used. Perhaps they are typical instances and perhaps they are not. I cannot say, for I am not at all sure how it could be shown either that they are typical instances or that they are not typical instances. And whether they are or are not typical instances is of no importance here. For all I wish to suggest is that at least one kind of situation where we use such descriptions is of the kind we have just mentioned. And if this is granted then that is quite sufficient for the purposes of this discussion.

One way of relieving the puzzle about the apparent 'conflict' between the first and fifth descriptions is to realize that we have a similar 'conflict' between the third and fourth descriptions. In one breath we can speak of two apples in the picture as being different sizes, one large and one small. In another breath we can also speak of the apples as being the same size, one in front of the other. We shall be in Alexander's dilemma if we feel that only one of these descriptions is the true description. If we feel inclined to say 'How can both of these accounts be true? Either the two apples pictured are the same size or they are not,' the same puzzle arises. For what shall we say? Shall we say the two apples are the same size but they look different? Or shall we say they are different sizes but they look alike? If we say they are the same size, in what way do they look different? Only in that one is close up and the other is off in the distance. When we say they are the same in size they also look the same size. If we say they are different in size, in what way do they look alike? For when we say they are different sizes we can also say they look different sizes. All that we shall have done, in introducing descriptions of how the apples look, is to have introduced another

pair of apparently 'conflicting' descriptions. For now instead of
the descriptions 'The apples are the same size' and 'The apples
are different sizes' we have the descriptions 'The apples look the
same size' and 'The apples look different sizes'. Thus we are not
one jot better off than we were at the start. (And this is one way
of seeing that the use of descriptions of what we see and how
things look is not germane to our problem.)

What we must realize here is that these apparently 'conflicting'
descriptions, the third with the fourth, the first with the fifth,
do not in fact conflict with one another. They could conflict
only if they were used in the same ways, in the same situation
and for the same purposes. This is not the case, and that it is not
must be quite clear. If we contrast the description 'The painting
is flat'—when we use this description to inform a carpenter about
the width of a crate required for shipping a painting, with the
description 'The painting has great depth'—when we use this
description to inform an art-critic about the structure of a painting, we can see that these two descriptions have nothing to do
with one another. It would be absurd to tell the carpenter
'The painting has great depth' for he would suppose a very wide
crate was required. And it would be equally absurd to tell the art-
critic 'The painting is flat' for he would be astounded to hear
that a Cézanne still-life had no depth. He might well reply 'Are
you sure? Cézanne was a master in his treatment of space.
Perhaps the painting is not an original?' If an art-critic tells us
'Many of Gauguin's paintings, unlike those of Cézanne, are flat',
are we to say the critic is confused? Doesn't he know that all
paintings are flat? And if we told this to the critic he would
probably reply in a justifiably irritable tone that he had no time
to waste on this nonsense. If we didn't learn enough about art
when we were children to understand what he is talking about
we had better go back to school and learn some more before we
attempt to philosophize about art.

The point is that the description 'The painting is flat' which
we use in speaking about a painting to an art-critic is totally
unlike the description 'The painting is flat' which we use in
speaking about a painting to a carpenter. If we do not take the
notion too seriously it is useful here to speak of a family of
descriptions; in this way we can speak of members of the

carpenter's family of descriptions, and members of the art-critic's family, members of the chemist's family, and so forth. Now it is very important to realize that quite often members of the carpenter's family look very much like members of the art-critic's family. We have already pointed out that the descriptions 'The painting is flat' and 'The painting has depth' which belong to the critic's family have their doubles which belong to the carpenter's family. And note that the descriptions 'The painting looks flat' and 'The painting looks as if it has depth' which belong to the carpenter's family also have their doubles which belong to the critic's family. And there are many other sets of doubles; e.g. 'The painting is top-heavy', 'The painting is fragile', and so forth, all have their doubles. But we ordinarily have no trouble in telling them apart. The reason for this is that they rarely associate. Members of the carpenter's family hardly ever stray into an art gallery for, if they do, they are usually thrown out by the critic who finds them dull company. The only time a member of the carpenter's family ever lingers in an art gallery is when he has been dragged in by the heels by some philosopher to be mated with a member of the critic's family. Is it any wonder that such a union engenders a contradiction? But this is no excuse for the philosopher to claim that the members of the critic's family are all bastards. When we say 'The painting is flat' and then in another breath add 'but the painting has great depth' we are mixing up these two, quite different, descriptions in a horribly confused manner so as to yield a dilemma. There is in fact no conflict between these two descriptions; thus there is no need to try to explain away one in favour of the other.

Of course, in saying there is in fact no conflict between these two descriptions I do not wish to suggest that every time someone says 'The painting is flat but the painting has great depth' it is necessarily the case that in fact there is no conflict. For this would be very much like saying that it is necessarily the case that no one in fact could contradict himself. And this certainly is not true. People are not in the habit of deliberately pronouncing explicit contradictions, but this is not to say that they could not do so if they chose. But the presumption is that if anyone does, in the ordinary run of things, say 'The painting is flat but it has great· depth' he is not deliberately pronouncing an explicit contradiction, but rather, is mixing up two, quite different, descriptions, perhaps deliberately, so as to yield an apparent paradox. In such a case there is in fact no conflict between these two descriptions and, thus, there is no need to attempt to explain away one in favour of the other. Even more significantly, there is no need, and indeed it is a serious mistake, to suppose that there is some unique object corresponding to each different description. It is an error, and an error which has vitiated a good deal of recent æsthetics, to postulate some illusory or imaginary object to be the work of art. The ordinary painting hanging in the museum is the work of art, and not some illusion or hallucination. There aren't two things being referred to when we say, in the carpenter's shop, 'The painting is flat', and when we say, in the gallery, 'The painting has great depth'. There is just one, and it is the painting. *There are two descriptions, not two objects.*

In concluding this paper I should like briefly to indicate one important point that we have not mentioned. And although we have not mentioned it, this point is quite important for there is very good reason to believe that it is the source from which all these other puzzles stem. To see just what this is, it is essential to notice that Alexander, along with other æstheticians, does not feel inclined to explain away the description 'The painting is flat' but he does wish to explain away the description 'The painting has great depth'. This is quite illuminating, for the fact that he does wish to explain away 'The painting has great depth' but does not wish to explain away 'The painting is flat' shows that he is troubled by the one description in a way that he is not by the other. Thus if we wish to get at the source of this difficulty, it is not sufficient to indicate, as we have done, that these two apparently conflicting descriptions do not in fact conflict and that they have totally different uses. What we must do is eliminate the difficulty æstheticians find in connexion with our use of the description 'The painting has great depth'. And this difficulty is, of course, how to settle disputes over whether or no a painting does have great depth, how to verify the statement 'The painting has great depth', and so forth. Thus I am saying that æstheticians who try to explain away the description 'The painting has great depth' do so because they are inclined to believe that a dispute over the depth of a painting cannot be resolved. That is, they are inclined to say that in such a situation there is nothing that can be done to settle the issue, that we cannot establish either that the painting does have depth or that it does not have depth. Thus, instead of saying 'The painting has great depth' they feel we should say, if we wish to speak properly, 'The painting seems to have great depth'. Thus the fundamental question is: can we verify that the painting has great depth? And the answer is that, of course, we can. However, I do not propose to argue this point here. The question has been mentioned only to indicate that it is a problem which must be dealt with before that ghost of æsthetics, the mysterious æsthetic object, can finally be laid to rest.